"*Raising a Modern-Day Knight* has equipped fathers around the world to raise godly, courageous, and successful sons and, in so doing, has saved countless young men from experiencing the emotional wounds suffered by so many of their peers. This book can do more for the well-being of a community than any government program."

  —THE HONORABLE MIKE HUCKABEE
    Governor of the State of Arkansas

"Robert Lewis does an excellent job of helping fathers visualize what it takes to guide our sons into true manhood. The power of using ceremonies to celebrate the growth of a boy into a man has proven invaluable to me in raising my sons."

  —J. D. GIBBS
    President, Joe Gibbs Racing

"The greatest gift a father can give a son is to show him what a real man looks like and then deliberately prepare him to become one himself. Robert Lewis has a proven plan for the process. There's a reason that *Raising a Modern-Day Knight* became a classic the first day it hit the shelves. It's a timely message for a timeless responsibility written by one of the finest life coaches in the country."

  —DR. TIM KIMMEL
    Author, *Raising Kids for True Greatness*

"Robert Lewis is the man of the hour. . . . He not only paints a vivid vision of manhood, but practically equips dads to pass on this noble vision to their sons. *Raising a Modern-Day Knight* is more than a book. It's a movement of men who are determined to be successful where it counts—in their relationship with their sons. This book will give you the tools you need to affirm masculinity in your sons and pass on a legacy that will guide them their entire lives. I promise you, this is the one book that your sons will be eternally grateful that you read and applied. Just DO IT!"

—DR. DENNIS RAINEY
President, FamilyLife

"I have had the privilege of knowing Robert Lewis for more than twenty years. One of the passions on his heart is preparing the next generation of young men to become mature, godly men. He has given to us in *Raising a Modern-Day Knight* a powerful, practical tool to help us raise our sons to become committed, noble men of God. This book is a treasure. Thank you, Robert, for this invaluable resource!"

—DR. CRAWFORD W. LORITTS, JR.
Author, speaker, senior pastor, Fellowship Bible Church, Roswell, Georgia

FOCUS ON THE FAMILY®

Raising a Modern-Day Knight

A Father's Role in Guiding His Son to Authentic Manhood

ROBERT LEWIS

TYNDALE

Tyndale House Publishers, Inc.
Carol Stream, Illinois

A Focus on the Family book published by Tyndale House Publishers, Carol Stream, Illinois 60188

Focus on the Family and the accompanying logo and design are federally registered trademarks of Focus on the Family, Colorado Springs, CO 80995.

TYNDALE and Tyndale's quill logo are registered trademarks of Tyndale House Publishers, Inc.

Editor: Colorado Wordmaster
Cover design by Paul Vorreiter, Jon Collins, Kirk Luttrell, and Mark Wainwright.
Produced with the assistance of The Livingstone Corporation.
Original family crest graphic by Nancy Carter

Library of Congress Cataloging-in-Publication Data
Lewis, Robert, 1949 Nov. 24-
  Raising a modern-day knight : a father's role in guiding his son to
authentic manhood / Robert Lewis.
      p. cm.
  Includes bibliographical references.
  ISBN: 978-1-58997-309-1
  1. Fathers and sons—Religious aspects—Christianity. 2. Child rearing—Religious aspects—Christianity. 3. Knights and knighthood—Miscellanea. I. Title.
  BV4846.L48 2007
  248.8'421—dc22

                                   2006026132

Printed in the United States of America
7 8 9 10 11 12 13 / 16 15 14 13 12

*To dads everywhere who desire to empower
their sons with a manhood of honor,
molded by the life of Jesus Christ.*

Contents

FOREWORD

Wow! Let me get right to the point. If you're a man, you need this book. And if you have a son, you *really* need this book. Frankly, our whole culture needs this book.

Every once in a while a volume comes along that stands alone, separating itself from the myriad of others coming off the presses like thousands of tiny aspirin tablets on a conveyor belt. *Raising a Modern-Day Knight* is such a standout book. I picked it up on New Year's Day before the games started. Now, I love football, but you would not have known it that day. Robert Lewis reached up out of the pages of this volume and thrust his message down into my chest with such captivating force that I forgot all about my favorite sport.

Emotion. Reflection. Instruction. Inspiration. Commission. It's all here. This is a great book because it's well written by a great man to address a great need. There is a passion in it—and a vision.

Here's why you need this book: Our culture is in deep trouble, and at the heart of its trouble is its loss of a vision of manhood. If it's difficult for you and me as adult males to maintain our masculine balance in this "gender-neutral" culture, imagine what it must be like for our young sons who are growing up in an increasingly feminized world. C. S. Lewis summed it up years ago when he stated that modernists "castrate and bid the geldings be fruitful."

We men are beginning to find the trail back. And we've got to show it to our sons. The Bible provides an absolutely accurate map, and Robert Lewis has helped us calibrate our compasses. *Raising a Modern-Day Knight* is a magnificent field manual for fathers who want to see their sons become men. Real men. Godly men.

Just how does a boy become a man? It certainly doesn't "just happen" anymore . . . if it ever did. What is a man? What processes produce such a man? And how do you know when you've become a man? These three questions are critical. You'll find the answers to all three between the covers of this book. Where does a young man go to become a man of strength, heart, conviction, and vision? He ought to be able to go to his dad! Boys become men by emulating older men, especially their fathers.

Let me tell you just a word about Robert Lewis. I've known him for more than 20 years, and I trust him. Every now and then you come across a man you could "ride the river with." Robert Lewis is such a man. He is a man of strength, heart, conviction, and vision. He has always been a leader—on the football field as a Division I linebacker . . . in the church as a pastor of a dynamic, growing, and influential church . . . and across the country as a nationally recognized speaker and author addressing critical family issues.

Robert Lewis has given fathers a magnificent, manly curriculum for turning boys into men. It is, by far, the finest I've seen. There is clear definition . . . and thoughtful process . . . and invigorating ceremony. As always, with Robert, the material is rock-solid biblical and intensely practical. I wish I'd had this book 20 years ago. I'm glad you've got it in your hands now. Devour it.

Stu Weber
Gresham, Oregon

Introduction

It begins as a typical Saturday morning. You're enjoying your second cup of coffee while reading the newspaper. Suddenly, you notice your son in a new way. He doesn't know you're watching him, but in this special, reflective moment, you realize *he's growing up*. I mean, *really* growing up.

Like never before, it becomes obvious to you that the contours of childhood are starting to disappear. Look at him! There's real hair on those legs! A muscular physique is emerging. You're beginning to see "the man" in him.

But what kind of man?

This is one of the most important questions of our day, because it targets a process missing in many homes. How does a boy grow into a man? A real man? A godly man? One with character, conviction, and vision? Where does he go to find a manly sense of himself? Who confers upon him the title and responsibilities of manhood?

If questions like these scare you because you intuitively sense they are *your* responsibilities as a dad, join the crowd. When a mom asked me such questions years ago, expecting articulate answers because I was not only a father of two sons but also a "family expert," I stumbled badly. How *does* a son grow into a man? I didn't know.

But I determined then and there to find out. This soon became one of the most rewarding journeys of my life.

In sharing my discoveries here, my hope is that you will not only be joined in a more significant way to your sons, but also to other men in a special masculine bond.

You need to know, Dad, that your son and thousands like him are presently being stripped of their maleness by a modern, secular, feminist culture. Over the last few decades, this culture has steadily and relentlessly undermined healthy notions of what it means to be a man. Once-noble images of masculinity have now been replaced by images of men behaving badly . . . or incompetently . . . or both. Manhood is no longer a unique calling; it's now seen more as a problem to overcome.

At the same time, many young men are confused because of their *lack* of connection with their fathers—socially, emotionally, and spiritually. All this has created an acute masculine identity crisis. If you were to ask most young men today, "How does a man act?" or "What are his unique responsibilities?" or "What role should he assume in his marriage?" you would receive little more than a blank stare. Many have no concept of this kind of man they should become. Not a clue. Listen to the poem one young man penned for me out of his own personal manhood vacuum:

What is a man?
Is he someone who is strong and tall,
Or is taut and talented as he plays ball?
Is he someone who is hardened and rough,
Who smokes and drinks and swears enough?
Is he someone who chases women hard,
With a quest to conquer, but never dropping his guard?
Is he someone with a good business mind,
Who gets ahead of the others with his nose to the grind?
Or is he someone who tries his best,
Not really caring about any of the rest?
What is a man? Does anyone really know?
TELL ME!
Who is the prototype? To whom shall I go?

Dad . . . *your* son is asking those very questions right now as he grows up under you. In fact, many of the social problems of our day (plummeting morality, rising crime, violence, abuse, reckless pleasure-seeking) spring from the soil of directionless, disconnected sons.

Conversely, I believe a healthy, vibrant masculinity goes hand-in-hand with social stability. So, I feel hope when I see the work of movements such as Promise Keepers. It's obvious that many men today are searching again for their true masculine identity.

The *best hope* still lies in the hearts of fathers . . . in dads who are beginning to ask, "How can I raise my boy into a man? A real man?" These are the right questions from the one who is most naturally suited to give answers that will stick for a lifetime.

As I have presented to a number of fathers the ideas and practical how-to's offered in this book, the response has been instantaneously positive. *Dads want answers!* They want a process that calls their sons to be godly men. They want ceremonies that can celebrate their sons' passage from boy to man. We are all desperate for ideas and images that will help us empower our sons with masculine energy. We want to leave them a legacy of masculine health that will empower their families and communities of the next generation.

The question is *how?*

Hopefully, the answer is in your hands.

Part I

The Need for a Modern-Day Knighthood

Chapter I

Manhood: Don't Let Your Son Leave Home Without It

When I was a child,
I used to speak like a child,
think like a child, reason like a child;
when I became a man,
I did away with childish things.

—The apostle Paul, 1 Corinthians 13:11

D ad, try to imagine the following scenario. Your 18-year-old son is standing in front of you, tears welling in his eyes. In 30 seconds he will get into his car and drive away to college. Except for the occasional holiday and summer visits, he'll be gone. Forever.

Nervously, you reach out to wrap your arms around him. The touch of his flesh against yours releases a flood of emotions—in him as well as you.

And then the memories come.

You recall the day of his birth and how proud you were to have a son. You remember his first words, and his first hit in tee-ball—he ran to third base instead of first! You recall the fishing trips and holidays, the ties he gave you for Christmas, the cards you received on Father's Day, and the special way he looked out for his little sister.

The years have passed so quickly.

In that moment, between muffled sobs and nervous laughter, you realize what a fortunate man you are . . . to have a son like this.

The embrace ends. You and your boy brush the tears from your cheeks. You tell your son how proud you are of him. He says, "Dad, I love you." Then he turns around, gets in the car, and drives away.

But what does he drive away *with*? A few precious memories? An emotional good-bye? Or possibly, when your son leaves, will he know in his gut—like a select few—what it means to be a man?

REMEMBRANCES OF A SON

For decades, Sam Rayburn was arguably the most powerful politician in America. During his lengthy tenure as Speaker of the House of Representatives, presidents came and presidents went, but Rayburn remained at the center of power. Rayburn *alone* controlled the legislative process in Washington. No bill came to a vote without his approval; no president could expect to succeed without his support.

In later years, when Sam Rayburn looked back upon his illustrious career and recounted the most influential moments in his life, one experience stood out above the rest.

It occurred at a railroad station in East Texas, far removed—in both time and space—from the marbled halls of Washington. Throughout his life, Sam Rayburn would talk about this singular event with great joy and deep reverence. In fact, he recalled the moment, says biographer Robert A. Caro, "at every crisis in his life."[1]

On one particular day in 1900, surrounded by the windswept Texas prairie, Sam's dad had hitched the buggy and driven his 18-year-old son to town. The boy was going off to college and would be leaving the farm that his father, a poor man, had tilled his whole life. Standing together on the railway platform, father and son awaited the approach of the train. Sam's "suitcase"—actually, a bundle of clothes tied up with a rope—lay at his feet. No words were spoken.

Then, when the train arrived and Sam prepared to board, his father reached out and placed a fistful of dollars into his hand. Twenty-five dollars. According to Caro, "Sam never forgot that; he talked about that $25 for the rest of his life."

"Only God knows how he saved it," Sam would say. "He never had any extra money. We earned just enough to live. It broke me up, him handing me that $25. I often wondered what he did without, what sacrifice he and my mother made."

With tears in his eyes, Sam turned to board the train. Again his father reached out and grasped his hands. The four words he spoke would echo forever in the boy's memory. He said, simply, "Sam, be a man!"

A Blessing and a Dilemma

This memorable exchange between a father and son illustrates both a blessing and a dilemma.

The good side is obvious. In that one moment, Sam learned just

how much his father loved him. At life's most demanding and difficult times, Sam would look back and recall with fond affection his
father's sacrificial expression of love.

But the statement "Sam, be a man" presents a dilemma—not just
for Sam Rayburn, but also for every boy.

When *does* one become a man? Does it "just happen" when a boy
reaches puberty or when he leaves home? Does he achieve it when he
bags his first buck or drinks his first beer? Does it come with a driver's
license or with a diploma at graduation? Does it take a woman to help
him become a man?

And where do you fit into all of this, Dad?

In my estimation, fathers today are coming up short with their
sons at three critical points. First, we have failed to deliver to our sons
a clear, inspiring, biblically grounded *definition of manhood*. How critical is that? It's comparable to a hunter without a gun . . . or a soccer
game without a ball . . . or a cross-country trip without a map. Telling
a boy to "be a man" without defining manhood is like saying, "Be a
success." It sounds good. But, practically, it takes you nowhere.

Second, most fathers lack a *directional process* that calls their sons
to embrace the manhood they should be able to define. Typically,
what passes for masculine training in most homes is vague and hit-or-
miss. We assume sons will somehow "get it." But most don't. This hit-
or-miss pattern sends conflicting signals and suffers under the weight
of its own inconsistency. Worse still, it handicaps a son in knowing
how to move out of childhood and into manhood. What he really
needs is specific language and training that takes him to the place
where, like the apostle Paul, he can say, "When I became a man I did
away with childish things."

A third shortcoming involves the loss of *ceremony.* How many
dads today think of formally commemorating their son's progress or

passage into manhood? Very few. A pioneer of the secular manhood movement, Robert Bly, makes this penetrating observation: "There is no place in our culture where boys are initiated consciously into manhood."[2] Manhood ceremonies have, in fact, become a lost art form. And sons have lost these powerful, life-changing moments where, in the presence of Dad and other men, they can mark either their progress toward or passage into manhood. In the absence of these special ceremonies, sons are left to wonder, *Am I a man?*

Of course, it doesn't have to be this way. But if dads like you and me are going to have better outcomes, we must invest these three missing assets into our sons' manhood portfolios.

How much better would it have been if Sam Rayburn's father had fleshed out a definition of manhood years earlier? What if he had taken Sam through a process that enabled him to become a man? And what if, after Sam had completed the process, his father had sealed and certified his manhood with a ceremony?

Is there some way to introduce these three elements—a definition, a process, and ceremonies—into your son's life? Yes. And it begins by looking back to another day and another time for inspiration . . . back to the age of knights.

THE RELEVANCE OF KNIGHTHOOD

This medieval figure casts an impressive masculine shadow. Clothed in chain mail, brandishing a sword, and mounted on an invincible steed, the knight remains even today a powerful symbol of virile manhood.

Vestiges of knighthood still dot our cultural landscape, from our language to our ideals to our traditions. For example, when a woman speaks of "my knight in shining armor," she envisions a man of noble character, romantic sensibilities, and brave deeds. Our concept of the "gentleman" had its origins in the chivalric code of honor. Many military ceremonies and traditions were birthed in the kingly courts of thirteenth-century Europe. The U.S. Army's sports teams from West Point are stilled called "the Black Knights."

And who among us boys didn't thrill to the legends of King Arthur and the Knights of the Round Table? The knight survives in our collective consciousness like an ancient Superman, committed to a code of conduct that Tennyson summarized as "Live pure, speak true, right wrong, follow the King."[3]

Even though historians would probably say the knight once popularized by literature was more an ideal than a reality, still he remains a powerful metaphor. In fact, I will be so bold as to argue that knighthood—despite some of its shortcomings—offers to any dad a powerful outline for his son's successful journey to manhood.

What's even more encouraging is to remember that the light of knighthood arose in the suffocating moral darkness and social chaos of the rough-and-tumble Middle Ages. In that sense, knighthood provides for modern-day dads a *model of hope* for raising healthy sons with moral and spiritual vision, despite our own increasingly dark and crude culture.

THREE DADS WITH A MISSION

Two other dads and I fell upon this knighthood concept some years back as we wrestled with how to help our sons become the kind of men we and God would be proud of. It was natural for us to do so, in light of the many ways our lives had overlapped. Bill Parkinson, Bill Wellons, and I first met at the University of Arkansas during the late '60s. What brought us together was our common desire for spiritual

Bill Wellons, Robert Lewis, and Bill Parkinson

discovery and growth. As young Christians, we were in Campus Crusade for Christ together; Bill Parkinson was actually one of the staff members.

After graduation we went our separate ways, only to be brought back together in 1980. This time, we were pastors of a new church in Little Rock. As the years went by, we not only developed a special professional relationship, but a deep personal friendship as well.

By 1989, with seven sons now growing up underneath us, we began to feel an urgency to give them some clear masculine tracks on which to run. The growing cultural controversy and confusion about men in general, and men's roles in marriage and society in particular, sparked our initial discussions. So, too, did the rising passivity and irresponsibility we, as pastors, observed in the lives of more and more young men around us.

Our sons needed something more from us than just love and support. They needed help in becoming men. But what would that help look like? We were amazed at the lack of answers and resources available.

Take, for instance, that simple question we have already mentioned: "What is a man?" We found it immensely difficult to formulate an answer; it was like "trying to nail Jell-O to a wall." In time, however, our efforts paid off. We landed a definition we believe is clear, concise, and, more importantly, anchored by the weight of Scripture. (You will eat the fruit of our effort in Chapter 4, where our definition of manhood is set forth in detail.)

Another question was how to teach this concept of manhood to our sons in a way that would be life-changing. Someone suggested that we create a family crest to help present our manhood concepts symbolically. This crest could not only hang in each of our homes, but also be passed down to each of our sons. Having spent the previous summer in Poland on a missions trip, I had explored a number of castles and seen a number of knightly crests still hanging along the corridors.

So, our discussion went from crests to castles to . . . *knights,* and how one became a knight, and if knighthood could be used as an outline to move our sons to manhood. The answer we found was "Yes!"

What followed was a series of trial-and-error efforts that not only exceeded our expectations, but spawned new ideas. A whole manhood language evolved among us and our sons. We established special ceremonies to mark specific moments in our boys' journey to manhood. Puberty, for instance, became more than just a passing moment of physical transformation. It also became a key moment of manhood instruction and challenge, celebrated by a ceremony that would leave an unforgettable mark on each son as to who he was becoming and where he was going.

Other dads around us began to pick up on the things we were

doing. Without any persuasion on our part, they began to take our ideas and personalize them with their own sons. The feedback from these dads confirmed that their experiences were just as exciting as ours! Sons delight in knowing about manhood. In the sacredness of these manhood ceremonies, they bond with their dads in a way that must be experienced to be fully appreciated.

Sons need fathers who are involved in their lives—dads who will love them, teach them, and discipline them. But clearly, sons also need a masculine vision. They need a manhood language. They need a ceremony. And they need other men. Knighthood, as an outline, offers all this and more.

First, the knight *embodied a well-defined set of ideals.* Many knights sincerely adhered to and embraced a moral code of honor. They pledged themselves to their lord, their king, and their God. One historian writes:

> Honor was the shrine at which the knight worshipped: it implied renown, good conduct, and the world's approval. The "word of honor" was the most solemn oath the knight knew, and this alone became the reason for the most extravagant exploits.[4]

Many knights also became *milites Christi,* "Knights of Christ." As such, they believed they bore responsibilities to the kingdom of God and to society as a whole, not just to the lords they served. This chivalric code of honor formed the moral and social bedrock of noble life; it gave order and substance to an age otherwise in chaos and confusion.

As a symbol of manhood, a knight's chivalry points to one of the most pressing needs of young men in our generation: a well-defined set of ideals. Ideals set parameters; they shape a boy's identity and motivate him to higher levels of excellence, just as they did for the medieval knight. For a son, these ideals become a moral and spiritual beacon.

Unfortunately, nothing is more absent in our day than well-defined masculine ideals. Too many sons grow into adulthood cursed by the void of these "higher things" of manhood. Listen to what one young man wrote in a letter to me. It is a portrait, I believe, of what many young men inwardly feel about themselves:

> As I reflect back, even though my father was around me, I
> learned little of what it means to be a man. So how will I
> become one when, at age 29, I'm still questioning whether
> I know what it really means? Never in my life have I felt such
> a burden as that of the responsibility of being a "man" for my
> family. But what am I supposed to do? It puts me in a place
> where I'm left to figure all this out somehow. Where can I find
> a man to be an example for me of real masculinity? I don't
> know.

In Part II of this book—"The Knight and His Ideals"—I will assist you, as a father, in formulating three specific ideals for your son: a vision for manhood, a code of conduct, and a transcendent cause. As I mentioned, I'll answer the critical question "What is a man?" in Chapter 4 and then give you practical suggestions for implementing this answer in your boy's life.

There is a second reason why the medieval knight speaks to the modern boy's journey to manhood. Just as his chivalry embodied a well-defined set of ideals, his life also *outlined a well-defined process.* The boy who pursued knighthood followed a clearly marked path.

At age seven or eight, he became a page. He was removed from his mother's care and went to live in a castle, usually with an overlord or relative.[5] Here, the page learned about armor and weapons and falconry, the rudiments of knighthood. He also performed household tasks for the "queen of the castle."

At the age of 14, the page became a squire. He attached himself to a knight and traveled everywhere in his company, serving him in the most menial of tasks: He carried the knight's lance, woke him in the morning, and even helped him dress. The squire also competed in tournaments and perfected the skills he had learned as a page. Such rigorous discipline prepared him for the final stage of his journey.

When he turned 21, he was eligible for knighthood. An elaborate initiation, which included a night-long vigil, a ceremonial bath, and a dubbing, marked the completion of the process. He was now . . . *a knight!* He took his place in the order of knighthood and pledged himself to uphold the code of honor.

From page to squire to knight—a young man could envision the process, count the cost, and pursue his dream. Sadly, for a boy today, there is no equivalent path on the journey to manhood. There are no landmarks or milestones to guide a boy's journey and no ceremonies to tell him when manhood begins. With all of the discussion today on the subject of manhood, there remains a great void.

In Part III, I will address four specific stages that you, as a dad, can put to use. In fact, I will refer to them in Chapter 8 as "The Page Stage," "The Squire Stage," "The Knight Stage," and "The Promise/Oath Stage." Each offers a specific opportunity for you to challenge and instruct your son in a special way. Each builds upon previous one. Each leads him toward godly manhood.

Part III also captures a third characteristic of ancient knighthood: *ceremonies.* Becoming a medieval knight required rigorous training, but it also was sealed in an elaborate ceremony that was powerful and unforgettable. In Part III—"The Knight and His Ceremonies"—I will describe a number of memorable ceremonies for celebrating your own son's journey to manhood. I will also suggest one you can use to celebrate his becoming a man.

In Part IV—"The Knight and His Round Table"—I speak to the importance of including other men in a son's march to manhood. It is in a chorus of masculine voices (not just Dad's alone) that a son recognizes his noble call. "In abundance of counselors there is victory," the Scripture says (Proverbs 11:14). I have found, with great delight, a "victory" for our sons in the abundance of other men calling them to manhood.

Finally, in Part V—"The Knight and His Legacy"—I come back to you, Dad. There you will discover the vital role that integrity—your integrity—plays in your son's life.

"Not all knights were great men," writes R. A. Brown about the Normans, "but all great men were knights."[6] Chivalry exacted a heavy toll upon its followers; it demanded submission, obedience, and courage. But it gave to the world knights and, in the words of Will Durant, one of the "major achievements of the human spirit."[7]

I believe it is time to resurrect the chivalrous knight: his *ideals*, his *process*, and his *ceremonies*. I want him to speak to a new generation that also has the potential for greatness but lacks only the opportunity: our sons!

A FINISHED PROCESS

I remember when Bill, Bill, and I finished the last of our four manhood ceremonies with the first of our seven sons. We had already determined that this last ceremony would take place before their weddings. Bill Parkinson's son, Ben, had beaten the rest of the boys to the altar, so we planned his ceremony to occur at the conclusion of the rehearsal dinner.

I am not sure what the hundred or so guests thought of our public ceremony. We did offer a brief explanation of our years together mentoring Ben. Then we three dads stood before a beloved son and rehearsed back to him the commitments he had made to us and to God years earlier in his "becoming a man" ceremony. Ben had not departed his homestead, like Sam Rayburn, with "Be a man!" ringing in his ears. On the contrary, he had left home knowing he *was* a man! He had been initiated by us into manhood and its responsibilities years before.

As our ceremony continued, we each offered Ben a special word of wisdom for this new "Promise/Oath Stage" of life. Our personal comments—"swords of the masculine spirit," we call them—were intended to arm him for another campaign of honorable living.

We finished our ceremony by presenting to Ben and his bride-to-be, Aimee, a family crest. A similar crest has hung in each of our families' homes for many years. It has become a sacred item. It contains, symbolically, all the manhood messages with which we, as dads, had sought earnestly to empower our sons. Now, in this last ceremony, we invited Ben to come and stand with us as we presented to him a crest of his own. For this son, our manhood process was now complete. The final challenge was for Ben to pass these masculine truths on to the next generation.

Manhood . . . don't let your son leave home without it, Dad.

As I left the rehearsal dinner that evening, my mind went back to another wedding day I remember so well—my own. What a startling contrast between that moment and the one I had just experienced. Let me share it with you.

Chapter 2

The Invisible Dad

The most urgent domestic challenge facing
the United States at the close of the
twentieth century is the re-creation of
fatherhood as a vital social role for men.
—David Blankenhorn, *Fatherless America*

Two pictures summarize my relationship with my father. The first appears on the following page. It's my wedding day, December 28, 1971, in my hometown of Ruston, Louisiana. The immediate family has been quickly summoned at the reception for one last series of shots before Sherard and I dash off to our honeymoon.

So . . . what's wrong with the picture? Everyone looks pleasant enough.

But something is definitely amiss here, and my half of the family

My wedding in 1971. On the left, Sherard's parents, Bill and Helen Thompson; center, Sherard, me, and my mom, Billie Lewis; at right, my brothers Charles (left) and John.

was feeling it deeply that winter afternoon. Do you see it? That's right—my dad is missing.

Where was he on his son's wedding day? Or the night before, at the rehearsal dinner?

Dad was at home, drunk. The pressure of this celebration was too much for him. And whenever the pressure built up, my dad took his fears, his responsibilities, and his self-respect to his old friend—alcohol.

I think I must have been about 10 when I became aware that something was terribly wrong with Dad . . . and with my parents' marriage. I can't count the number of times my brothers, John and Charles, and I watched our inebriated father stumble through the house, with Mother reciting his failures at the top of her lungs. Every time it happened, something inside of me would die toward my dad. That's a terrible feeling for a young boy.

Christmas was always a particularly difficult time of year. Dad literally drank himself through the holiday season. I remember once how Mother wanted to gather us together to read the Christmas story from the Bible; we weren't a religious family, but she felt we should do something to celebrate Jesus' birth. As on so many other occasions, Dad resisted and the tension began to mount. He began drinking, and eventually the scene ended with three confused little boys sitting by the tree, watching Mom and Dad go at each other.

Sometimes we couldn't keep the embarrassment inside our four walls. I recall going to a downtown hardware store to pick up some nails for a backyard table Dad was working on. Several of the men there knew my dad and asked what the nails were for. When I told them, one said, "Tommy Lewis doesn't know anything about building something like that." Another quickly added, "But he sure knows a lot about the bottle!"

They all laughed, but I was fighting-mad furious. An instinctive father-son loyalty within me wanted to stand up and shout back, *You can't talk about my dad that way!* Unfortunately, they could. And all I could do was hurt and retreat inside myself.

As I moved into my teenage years, Dad's drinking became worse. I, more than my brothers, became the "in-house mediator" trying to keep the peace. I would go back and forth between my parents, trying to help them understand each other. It was an impossible task for a boy, and in the end it only made me the enemy of both.

You swallow a lot of pain when at 15 you tell your dad not to come out of his room until your friends are gone. You swallow a lot of pain hiding car keys or disposing of hidden whiskey bottles before the weekend comes. You swallow a lot of pain refereeing fights to make sure no one gets injured.

The Father We Never Had

The worst part, however, was not the alcohol. It was what we missed because of Dad's dependence on Jim Beam, Jack Daniels, Old Crow, and other liquors. We missed *him!* We missed feeling his heart, his closeness, his affirmation. We missed hearing his teaching, seeing his conviction, experiencing his *leadership!* Words like these should naturally go hand-in-hand with the word *Dad*. But he traded them all for alcohol. For my brothers and me, the word *Dad* felt more like shame, pain, and embarrassment—an unbearable incongruity.

My dad worked hard. He provided for our family, materially. We were a solid, middle-class family. And I do have a number of pleasant memories from my boyhood. But when my dad walked in the door at the end of a long day, his personal influence began to fade. As in the movie *The Invisible Man*, my dad would shed his corporate identity at home and begin to disappear altogether. He became "The Invisible Dad."

We rarely played together. In fact, I struggle to remember any time we threw the ball or wrestled together. I missed the fun side of him.

He never told me, "I love you." I never prayed with him or talked with him about spiritual things. I never knew what he believed. His inner world was a mystery to me. We never sat together and talked about life or girls or sex or school or the future. There was no fatherly preparation for things ahead.

I never heard him say, "I'm proud of you." I never experienced a moment when he shared with me what he thought I would be good at or what my responsibilities were as a man. He offered no measuring sticks to my life.

He had little to say at certain crucial moments in my life. When a host of college football scholarships were offered to me, his only com-

*At home with my brothers John (left) and Charles
(second from left), and my dad (right)*

ment was, "It's your decision." Everything was on my own . . . alone.

Dad's passivity with all of us was deafening. The lack of his direction was heartbreaking. My brothers and I were left to our own pathetic resources and guesswork for navigating ourselves through adolescence and early adulthood. And none of us did it very well.

THE MAN IN THE SHADOWS

There is a second picture that captures my life with Thomas Lewis, and perhaps you can relate to it. Maybe you didn't suffer the *dysfunction* I've already described, but you know the *distance* I am going to recall for you now.

This photograph was taken in 1970. I was home from college, my older brother, Charles, (in the middle) was home from the navy, and

John (in front) was living at home. Soon we would be heading in our own directions again as young men, and Mom decided to take a photo of all the Lewis men.

As you can see, we are standing shoulder-to-shoulder in the backyard, squinting in the bright sunlight. Where is Dad? He's behind us, the man with the dark shadow falling over his face.

What a case of art imitating life!

Dad dwelt in the shadows of our family all our lives. He was always a mystery to us . . . hard to see, hard to feel, hard to draw life from.

In fact, some years later, someone asked me, "How do you remember your dad?" For several long minutes, I sat with a mental blank. I couldn't think of anything to say. I have since come to understand why. The thought of Dad in any specific sense was just too painful.

THREE DIFFERENT ROADS

After that sunny day in 1970, the Lewis brothers headed in three different directions. John eventually moved to the Wyoming mountains to "find himself." My older brother, Charles, acutely felt the turmoil of my parents' marriage and the emotional disconnection from Dad. As time revealed, it shook the very foundations of his life. In his pain, he not only broke with Dad; he separated from masculinity altogether.

Years later, he would openly declare himself a homosexual and become an active part of the gay community where he lived. He came to believe he was born with this identity, discounting his woundedness growing up. At any rate, it would be the identity he would carry to his grave in 1988, when he died of AIDS.

I compensated for the lack of affirmation from Dad by seeking it from others through achievements. I excelled in sports and leadership, and earned a football scholarship to the University of Arkansas.

Two special people made a difference in my life during these years. The first was my high school football coach, L. J. "Hoss" Garrett. He became a masculine mentor. He gave me years of much-needed affirmation and encouragement. He cheered for me. He saw potential in me and would often tell me, "Robert, you're a leader. Reach high! Make a difference! I believe in you." For this rich investment, I later named my first son after him.

The second man and mentor to come into my life was Jesus Christ. I met Him in a powerful way the spring semester of my freshman year at college in 1968. Several Christian friends and a solid local church helped me nurture that relationship with deep roots in the Scriptures.

What Christ has done in my life since then is nothing short of miraculous. So many adults today are still stuck in the patterns of dysfunction they learned as children. And yet, through the years, I've seen how Christ can transform a person from the inside out. I've received from Him the power and direction I needed. And in the Scriptures, I've discovered the true model for manhood.

THE REST OF THE STORY

Before I move on, I'd like to tell you one more story about my dad— a positive one! Just as I found peace, strength, and salvation in Christ, so did Thomas Lewis.

I was pastoring a church in Tucson, Arizona, and on one particular night a group of friends and I were talking about the power of prayer in our small group. We raised the question, "What is one thing you want to trust God for—but you think is absolutely impossible?"

For me, the answer was clear: for my father to receive Christ as his Savior. He had already rejected that invitation several times. Nevertheless, people took it upon themselves to pray that night that something would happen in my father's life to cause him to see his need for Christ.

That very night, back in Louisiana, my father was in a drunken state at home. He and my mother were yelling at each other when he announced that he was going to leave and drive someplace. This was their typical pattern: yell and leave.

However, what happened next was not typical at all. Mom, seeking to keep Dad from driving drunk, grabbed him by the arm, trying to hold him back. With a powerful shrug, he brushed her away and stormed out the door. Little did he know that when he pushed her away, she tripped and fell backward. Her head hit the edge of a marble coffee table, knocking a telephone to the floor—and breaking her neck.

She lay there alone for several hours until an operator came onto the line. Mom was able to tell the operator what happened, and soon an ambulance rushed her to the hospital. She would lay in traction, with pins protruding from her skull to stabilize her spine, for 10 weeks.

Dad stayed out all night and went straight to work the next morning. When friends found him there, they told him what happened. One can only imagine the guilt that exploded within my dad at this awful announcement. He responded by suffering a heart attack on the spot. Another ambulance, another trip to the hospital.

THE BLESSING

When word of all this reached me the next day in Arizona, I immediately caught a plane and flew back to Ruston. When I walked into my father's hospital room, I had no idea what to say.

Dad was groggy from the medication, and I soon realized he didn't know who I was—he thought I was a doctor. I asked how he was doing, and all he could say was, "I've done a horrible thing." For several minutes, he painfully recounted the events of the last 24 hours.

Suddenly, he began to reminisce about his three sons and what each was doing. When he talked about me, he talked about what a good son I was and how I was pastor of this "big church" (he exaggerated a bit!) out in Tucson.

I couldn't believe what I was hearing. After all those years of deafening silence, I finally was receiving from him a special moment of love and approval I had always longed for. He didn't know he was talking to me, but I realized that the Lord had arranged those circumstances to allow me to receive this special blessing from my father.

As we continued talking, Dad began to realize who I was. With tears, he confessed, "I've done a horrible thing. I need to go to hell." Here was a man who had ignored God for many years and finally he saw his need. I didn't even think before I replied, "Dad, there is that judgment, but there is also a thing called forgiveness in Christ."

For a solid hour I talked to him about the gospel and how he could receive forgiveness of his sins. And at the age of 70, Thomas Lewis finally found his Savior. The impossible had happened within a single day of the asking!

As you can imagine, Mom and Dad had a lot of tension to work through. Friends and even family members urged my mom to divorce him, saying, "How can you keep living with a chronic alcoholic who broke your neck?" Mine was the only voice urging her to give the marriage one last try, because I saw a glimmer of hope now that Dad had received Christ.

Dad moved out of the home for a year and pledged to earn his way back. He finally began to accept responsibility for his life. He gave up drinking, received professional counseling, and worked to regain Mom's trust. Eventually he did return home.

I would be lying if I said all was well after that, because it wasn't. Bad habits die hard. But Dad and Mom stuck together and, in time, finally realized some peace in their lives after so many years of warfare.

MOVING BEYOND GOOD INTENTIONS

My life stands as a testimony to the fact that God can rebuild a legacy of manhood despite growing up with an invisible father. I also know I am an *exception*. Invisible Dads are toxic to their sons. I know because I have counseled many of them. Invisible Dads are busy, rushed, and full of good intentions. Their stories and circumstances vary widely, but the crippling impact of their lives upon their sons is the same: a disfigured masculinity with disastrous results.

No son should have to follow the path I walked. Every son deserves a dad who fills his life with love, affirmation, and blessing. Every son needs from his father vision, direction, and solid answers to questions such as:

• What is a man?
• What are a man's responsibilities?
• What does a man believe?
• How does a man behave?
• What should a man try to achieve?

These are the most important questions in a boy's life. And by God's grace, I now have the privilege of answering them for my sons. I intend to use my hurt for their gain. I intend to make sure the curse of the Invisible Dad goes no further than me.

How about you?

CHAPTER 3

THE DRIFT OF SONS

Experience has shown us that men
who are the happiest and most content
in their masculine role today are those
whose fathers invested a great deal of
time and energy in their lives.

—DAVID STOOP AND STEPHEN ARTERBURN, *THE ANGRY MAN*

I was casually watching *NBC Nightly News* one evening when up
came a surprising, 20-second story about—of all things—Jeffrey
Dahmer's brain. Yes, his brain.

You remember Jeffrey Dahmer, the man convicted in Milwaukee
back in 1992 for murdering and dismembering 17 people. Sentenced
to prison for 957 years, Dahmer was murdered by a fellow inmate two
years later. It seemed now that Dahmer's grey matter had been pre-
served for science, and it was creating controversy within his family.

Jeffrey's parents were split over what to do with it. Dahmer's mother wanted the brain studied to determine if Jeffrey was biologically predisposed to violence. His father wanted it buried, or destroyed, or whatever else you do with the brain of a serial killer.

Since the hideous details of Dahmer's crime became public back on July 23, 1991, Lionel Dahmer has searched his soul to understand his boy's macabre behavior. He wrote a book, *A Father's Story*, attempting to piece together the eerie events of Jeff's life.

A Father's Story tells a grievous tale. Lionel Dahmer could have included photographs of Jeffrey's mangled victims, but they wouldn't have had nearly the impact of the simple, innocent photographs of Jeff's childhood. A picture appears every 30 pages or so: Jeffrey as a toddler, giggling in his father's arms; Jeffrey, age four, playing in the backyard at his grandparents' home; Jeff and his buddy, Lee, dressed up for Halloween. Jeff was a handsome boy, with a broad smile and a shy demeanor, not unlike thousands of other little boys.

But something went wrong with Jeffrey Dahmer. Something horrible.

The scene that emerges in *A Father's Story* is one of parental neglect and domestic conflict: a wife struggling with loneliness and depression, a father consumed with graduate work—too busy to participate in his son's life. In this sterile environment, devoid of affection and attention, Jeffrey Dahmer did what many other boys do (though the vast majority never become serial killers). He started to drift. Lionel Dahmer writes:

> And so I wasn't there to see him as he began to sink into himself.
> I wasn't there to sense, even if I could have sensed it, that he
> might be drifting toward that unimaginable realm of fantasy and
> isolation that it would take nearly thirty years to recognize.[1]

To me those are haunting words.

I wasn't there.

He began to sink into himself.

He might be drifting.

Without even knowing it, Lionel Dahmer has identified a process that is confirmed by experience and verified by observation: *When Dad is absent, boys begin to sink into themselves. They begin to drift.* As Bronislaw Malinowski wrote in a *National Review* article, "Through all societies there runs a rule that the father is indispensable for the full sociological status of the child. . . . The most important moral and legal rule is that no child should be brought into the world without a man . . . who is guardian and protector."[2]

Our culture is convulsing today because, in the words of David Blankenhorn, we have undertaken a social experiment "of the most daring and untested design. It [fatherlessness] represents a radical departure from virtually all of human history and experience."[3] Only fathers can halt the drift of sons.

"GRANDCHILDREN ARE THE CROWN OF OLD MEN . . ."

Why does a father's absence portend such grave consequences for sons? The answer lies in the unique, divine design of the father-son relationship. No passage of Scripture captures this better than Proverbs 17:6: "Grandchildren are the crown of old men, and the glory of sons is their fathers."

The typical grandparent is a sentimental, fawning, ingratiating mass of elderly protoplasm. If you didn't know better, you'd assume that God created grandparents for the singular purpose of spoiling kids. Novelist Victor Hugo put it best: "There are fathers who do not love their children; there is no grandfather who does not adore his grandson."[4]

The writer of Proverbs is saying essentially the same thing. But he uses a word sparkling with symbolism to get his point across— "crown."

A crown means little to those who reside in a democracy. But ancient readers, living under monarchies, understood it immediately. To say that "grandchildren are the *crown* of old men" stresses a grandfather's feeling of honor and delight. Much like a coronation, the word symbolizes achievement and a sense of completion. This word lays open a grandfather's heart and shows us how he *feels* in the presence of his grandchildren. To put it simply, he feels like a king!

". . . And the Glory of Sons Is Their Fathers"

The Hebrew word translated "glory" in Proverbs 17:6 is *thephara*. The basic idea is "beauty" or "glory," but in this particular instance *thephara* refers to the act of "boasting."[5]

The writer is telling us that as grandchildren are to old men, so a father is to a son: a source of wonderment and delight . . . a reason for boasting. A son wants to feel like a *champion* in the presence of his dad.

This admiration is innate, not learned. Sons have an inherent desire to boast in front of their fathers. You've probably never heard a boy brag about his mother's cooking; it's always "My dad is stronger than your dad!" This father may be only five feet three and weigh 100 pounds dripping wet. But to his son, he's the Incredible Hulk.

Every dad begins fatherhood clothed in garments of praise. It usually happens naturally and effortlessly. He possesses an authority that is both inexplicable and awesome. For this reason, few things are more important to a boy—or a man—than a touch, or a smile, or a word of encouragement from Dad.

Bo Jackson, the former baseball and football star, is a prime example. In *Sports Illustrated*, Jackson made this painful admission:

> My father has never seen me play professional baseball or football. . . . I tried to have a relationship with him, gave him my number, said, "Dad, call me. I'll fly you in." Can you imagine? I'm Bo Jackson, one of the so-called premier athletes in the country, and I'm sitting in the locker room and envying every one of my teammates whose dad would come in and talk with them after the game. I never experienced that."[6]

A few years ago, a friend of mine saw this same desire for sons to be affirmed by their fathers when he spoke at a FamilyLife Marriage Conference in Alaska. Dan Jarrell told the men they needed to tell their children how much they loved them. At the end of the talk, one man came forward and handed Dan a slip of paper. It said:

> Dear Dan,
>
> My father was killed in World War II when I was three years old. I knew in my heart that he loved me; my mother told me that he loved me. But I always longed to hear it myself, from him.
>
> When my mother and stepfather retired and left Alaska, I came over one day to help them pack. Mom took an old army photograph of my father in his army uniform off her dresser and gave it to me. She said, "Here, this is for you. I know your father would have wanted you to have it." It was the same photograph I had seen for many years. As I took the picture

from her, I dropped it; the cheap metal frame hit the floor and broke, shattering the glass. Sick at heart, I reached down to salvage what was left of this family treasure. Behind the photograph I found a letter, placed there 37 years before and long since forgotten. It was a letter from my father to his three-year-old son, the last letter he had written before he died. In it he said that he loved me and that he longed to come home and be with me.

I had heard the words I needed to hear from a father who was long since dead.

Why did this man yearn to hear his father say "I love you," and why was he so excited to share it with Dan? *The glory of sons is their fathers.* Why does an unkind word from Dad pierce a young man's heart? *The glory of sons is their fathers.* Why does a three-year-old boy run joyfully into his father's arms at the end of the day? *The glory of sons is their fathers.* Why did Bo Jackson ache for his father's attention? *The glory of sons is their fathers.*

MASCULINE MOORINGS

Something about a father's physical and emotional presence gives life to a boy. Masculine life. Just being around dad—watching him shave, hearing him laugh, touching his flesh—invests a son with large doses of male energy. And this emotional capital cannot be gained anywhere *other* than in the presence of a father.

The investment becomes even more substantial when a father imparts not only emotional capital, but moral and spiritual capital as well. In this nurturing environment, a son is weighted down with a masculine anchor. He lashes his soul to masculine moorings. But this also explains why sons drift in the *absence* of fathers. Instead of being weighted down, they become weight*less.*

"*I wasn't there . . .*"

"*He began to sink into himself . . .*"

"*He might be drifting . . .*"

I've met every Wednesday morning with more than 400 men from our church and community for something called "Men's Fraternity." Begun back in 1989, this group's inaugural meetings covered basic theology and issues relevant to spiritual life. Over 100 men turned out each week at 6:00 A.M. to probe these topics.

One day in 1991, I decided to devote Men's Fraternity to the subject of manhood. When nearly 300 guys showed up, I realized I had hit a nerve. The atmosphere that first day was electric. It was clear that these men had a desperate need to discover true masculinity.

As I met with many of these men and heard their stories, I also heard a sad refrain, much like the chorus of a dirge. The faces changed, but the words remained the same. Through heartache and tears, often squeezed out in muffled sobs, man after man repeated the words "My dad wasn't there for me."

Somewhere along the way, their hero had let them down. The glory inherent in a dad in the beginning had tragically faded. What remained was not glory but pain.

A REVOLUTION OF FATHERHOOD

Thankfully, our culture is now awakening to the importance of fatherhood. One of the most promising rediscoveries of our generation is that fathers matter. Publishers have been cranking out books with titles like *Wisdom of Our Fathers, The Father Factor, The Difference a Father Makes, Why a Son Needs a Dad,* and *Why a Daughter Needs a*

Dad. Men are attending conferences to become better husbands and fathers. Dads who grew up in the absence of fathers are committing themselves to their children.

A cultural revolution has begun. What college students were to the '60s, what women were to the '70s, and what yuppies were to the '80s, dads may yet be to this generation. Fathers are coming home.

The revolution transcends religious, racial, and ethnic boundaries. Even some of the most hard-boiled men are making their families a priority, like rock 'n' roll star Bob Seger, who said:

> I've just changed my whole value system; I know what's important. I want to be a good dad. I want to be a good husband. That's my top priority. And if I can still do my work well, great.[7]

All of this bodes well for our society, if it sticks. The transformation can't come too soon. For too long fathers have been lost in the wilderness, pursuing careers and pleasures at the expense of their children.

GIVING THE "BEST THINGS"

But a father's presence is not all that's required to cure a son's drift. Listen very closely. Something *more* is needed than a father's "interest" and "involvement," as good as these are. My fear is that as dads come home and as the men's movement goes forward, we will make the mistake of giving our sons *good* things, but not the *best* things. Let me explain.

Some time ago I taught a class for parents at our church entitled "Morally Empowered Teens." I began one session by asking fathers a series of questions. First, I asked if they were involved in their sons' activities: things like athletic events, school programs, and church.

Virtually every hand in the room shot into the air.

I then asked these fathers if they helped with homework. Again, I received a fairly strong response.

Next, I said, "Are you imparting a biblical vision for manhood to your sons?" No one raised a hand.

I then asked if they were training their sons to relate to the opposite sex—not just sexually but socially. Had they explained a man's role with a woman from a biblical perspective? No response.

Finally I asked if they had some specific masculine values in mind for their boys—godly, noble values. A few hands, ambiguous and tentative, went up. Meanwhile, most men dropped their eyes to the floor. They were embarrassed.

In that moment, I discovered a flaw in our approach to fatherhood. We're giving our sons *good* things, but not the *best* things.

In his book *Fathers and Sons,* Dr. Lewis Yablonsky states, "A man in his role of father delivers a basic philosophical message to his son."[8] The question I ask is, what message are fathers—even the best fathers—delivering to their sons today? What values are we communicating to the next generation?

Read carefully, for sociologist Allan Bloom has the answer:

> Fathers and mothers have lost the idea that the highest
> aspiration they might have for their children is for them to
> be wise—as priests, prophets or philosophers are wise. Special-
> ized competence and success are all that they can imagine.[9]

What is missing today in most father-son relationships? Why do the sons of even good, emotionally involved fathers drift in adulthood? Because we have forgotten to give them *the best things!* A social and spiritual competence can be summarized in three phrases:

A vision for manhood

A code of conduct

A transcendent cause

These are the building blocks of real manhood!

We will explore these supreme gifts in great detail in Chapters 4-6. But for now, let us realize that sons can drift not just because "Dad wasn't there for me," but also because "Dad forgot to give me the best things." One man put it this way to me: "My father hugged and loved us, but he didn't provide a road map for life. He just let it happen."

Hang-loose fatherhood, no matter how loving, is not an acceptable answer for today's young men. They need something more to keep them from losing their way.

Sons are looking for the substance of life. As I hope to prove, they hunger for the *best things*. In the absence of these anchors, sons drift. But when loving dads add these into the manhood mix, their sons flourish. They become noble men, gentle men, men of valor, principled men, *knights*.

Part II

The Knight and His Ideals

CHAPTER 4

A Vision
for Manhood

What then is chivalry? So strong a thing,
And of such hardihood, and so costly in the learning,
That a wicked man or low dare not undertake it. . . .
Whoso would enjoy high honor first must suitably
Display that he has well been schooled in such arts.

—*The Biography of William Marshall*

K ing Philip II of France was dining with dignitaries when a messenger entered the royal chamber. He bore ill tidings.

The courier spoke softly to Philip, furtively shielding the news
from curious ears. As the king strained to listen, watchful guests
detected a look of sadness in his eyes. Their interest was piqued, but

they said nothing. They knew it was inappropriate to inquire of an earthly sovereign. Minutes passed.

Finally, the king turned toward his friend, Guillaume des Barres, and said, "Have you heard what this messenger has told me?"

"What is it?" responded Barres.

"By my faith," replied the king, "he has come to tell me that William, the Earl of Pembroke, is dead and buried."

Silence fell upon the gathered nobility. Slowly, reverently, voices began to speak out in praise of William Marshall. Their admiration was devout and sincere; it arose from hearts well acquainted with the bravery of William's deeds and the content of his character. Said Jean de Rouvray, an intimate of King Philip: "Sire, I judge that this was the wisest knight that was ever seen, in any land, in our age."

Then it was left to the king to summarize the group's sentiments. He said simply, "William Marshall was, in my judgment, the most loyal man and true that I have ever known, in any country I have been."[1]

That's a powerful tribute for any friend. But what made this compliment so powerful was that it was a tribute to an enemy! King Philip was a Frenchman, William Marshall an Englishman.

William Marshall's life is a study in chivalry. For good reason, contemporary historians regard him as the ideal knight. One incident serves to illustrate his courage. In May 1197, Marshall's band of knights attacked the castle of Milli, near Beauvais in France. They placed ladders against the wall and began to swarm into the garrison.

But the defenders were not idle. One ladder was thrown down, hurling its load of knights to the ground. Before the ladder fell, however, a knight named Guy de la Bruyere was caught about his neck by a great fork used by one of the defenders and was held, helpless.

William, who was directing the attack, saw the knight's predicament. By himself, he climbed the ladder again and fought to free his fellow knight. When the defenders fled, William found that he now controlled that section of the wall. His men cheered, "The castle is taken! To his aid!"[2]

Marshall's heroics proved the difference in the battle. Similar acts of valor were repeated many times throughout the course of his life.

But bravery was not his only trait. He was also a devout family man. In an age that was largely indifferent to children, the rich baron made provision for each of his 10 children, fretting endlessly over his youngest daughter, who was unmarried at the time. Of his relationship with his wife, Isabel, biographer Georges Duby informs us that he watched over her "as over the most precious treasure in the world."[3]

He was an exceptional man in an enigmatic age.

The historian who seeks to understand the formation of such strong character quickly recognizes two significant influences: *a powerful mentor* who shaped William Marshall's life, and *a particular kind of culture* that offered a clear path to manhood. At an early age, Marshall was apprenticed as a page to his first cousin William of Tancarville, chamberlain of the king of England. In the presence of this nobleman, through childhood and adolescence, young Marshall acquired the tools and the spirit of knighthood. So impressive was this apprenticeship upon the boy's psyche that he "kept upon him the sign [crest] of the family where he had trained, which had made him a man. He displayed it like a warrant, a patent of quality."[4]

HARNESSING THE PASSION OF MASCULINITY

Medieval culture also shaped William Marshall's masculine identity. Despite its well-documented barbarities, the virtuous side of medieval society provided him with something sorely lacking in our day—a clear, distinct vision of manhood. Training boys from an early age, imparting a code of conduct, and marking their progress with ceremony and celebration ensured that adolescents became men. The unrestrained passions of masculinity, which can tear at the fabric of society, were harnessed mostly for good, not for evil.

Modern culture does little to harness the energy and passions of men for good. This may well explain why men are responsible for much of our social upheaval. For example:

- In 2002, 88 percent of local jail inmates were men.
- In 2001, 93.4 percent of state prison inmates were men.
- In 1997, 93 percent of federal prison inmates were men.
- In 1996, 92 percent of convicted, violent felons were men.

The lifetime chance that a person will go to prison is 1.8 percent for women, 11.3 percent for men.[5]

Boys become men in the presence of a clear vision for manhood. But as the writer of Proverbs notes, "Where there is no vision, the people are unrestrained" (29:18). Boys get out of control. And society suffers.

After a lifetime of studying cultures and civilizations, both ancient and modern, the eminent anthropologist Margaret Mead made the following observation: "The central problem of every society is to define appropriate roles for the men."[6] Author George Gilder adds: "Wise societies provide ample means for young men to affirm themselves without afflicting others."[7]

Psychologically, men are far more fragile than women. Men struggle with their identity much more than women do. Though feminists would have us believe that poor self-esteem is largely a female problem, caused primarily by social inequities, the evidence tells a different story. "Men, more than women," says David Blankenhorn, "are culture-made."[8] For this reason, a cultural definition of manhood is critical.

But where can a young man find a healthy, masculine identity—*a vision for manhood*—in today's culture? In the past, three sources usually provided solid answers.

Source #1: Community

Communities in the past possessed a shared vision of masculinity. They provided ceremonies to mark a boy's passage from adolescence to manhood.

For example, before fighting disrupted their region, the Nuer people of southern Sudan used extreme measures to initiate their young men into manhood. A boy was taken from his home and mother and brought into the community of men. He was made to lie down while deep cuts were made in his forehead; these represented the distinctive markings of a male warrior in the tribe.

After this painful initiation, the boy was never again permitted to sleep in his mother's home. He would join the men from that point on. He was now considered a man—qualified to fight, hunt, marry, and provide for a family. To this vision he would now aspire or be shamed.

If all of this sounds like a traumatic thing to put a boy through . . . *it is!* It is a shocking and painful—some would say egregious— experience that drives home an unforgettable message. The young man's psyche, as well as his body, have been forever marked with Nuer manhood.

For men in our culture, it is the absence of such a clear rite of passage that has led many of them into the woods—beating drums and dancing naked—in the hope of discovering who they are.

The Nuer boy could say, "Today, I became a man! I know who I am and what is expected of me." He could point to the marks on his forehead and the community ceremony to prove it.

But when does a boy become a man in *our* society? When he gets his driver's license? Or joins the army? Maybe when he takes a woman to bed? Or when he can provide financially for himself? Ask your community to tell you when a boy becomes a man, and the only answer you will receive is an awful silence.

You feel the ambiguity, don't you? With no community vision for manhood, boys are left to grapple with an amorphous identity.

SOURCE #2: FAMILY

Historically, Dad was a critical piece in the manhood puzzle. But in our age of absent fathers, this piece is missing. Gordon Dalbey writes:

> I see many men walking around in mid-life with a sense of yearning for things they can't get from their wives and can't get from their jobs, and can't pull from inside themselves. Having listened to thousands of stories in workshops around the world, I'm convinced that what men are missing is a sense of their own identity; a very primitive and very deep sense of validation that passes from father to son.[9]

I wonder: Did you get this deep sense of validation from your father? Did he fill up your masculine soul with affirmation and vision, or did he tear it down with distance and aloofness? Was his manhood clear to you? Is yours clear to your son? As we discussed in detail in Chapter 3, dads are the central component of any boy's manhood vision.

SOURCE #3: CHURCH

Entrusted with the sacred revelation of Scripture, pastors and theologians throughout the centuries have salted communities and families with images and concepts of authentic manhood. But sadly, under the assault of modern culture and feminist ideology in particular, these bold images of manhood—of masculine responsibilities and manly roles—have been silenced or reinterpreted.

Man, the "head" of a woman? "Who says?" cries the politically correct church. "Who *dares* to say?" The push for gender neutrality has gutted authentic manhood. Listen to *Wall Street Journal* columnist Walter Benjamin:

> As a child, I always accompanied my parents to church after Sunday School. As I looked up at the protective, strong, yet compassionate face of my father, I intuitively knew the church wanted to forge a link between the qualities of God and that of earthly fathers.
>
> But have you listened carefully to your church's liturgy recently? If so, God may be referred to as everything except Father.
>
> The very idea, that calling God "Father" has been harmful to women isn't merely wrong—it's dangerous. The sanitizers are actually destroying a divine measurement that has historically held husbands and their sons responsible.[10]

Nestled among the closing comments of Paul's first letter to the Corinthians is a short, stout admonition: "Be on the alert, stand firm in the faith, *act like men*" (1 Corinthians 16:13, emphasis added). In the cultural context in which it was offered, the phrase "act like a man" meant something definitive. Today, this same biblical phrase rings hollow. Why? Because today's church is retreating from, rather than filling, this growing vacuum.

THE TWO FOREMOST PERSONALITIES IN SCRIPTURE

Our day of confusion cries out for a rock-solid definition of manhood, the kind of definition that transcends the cultural confusion now washing over men today. But where do we find such a definition? As with all other significant issues in life, the Bible holds the key.

We can arrive at a rock-solid definition by comparing and contrasting two prominent Bible characters. In fact, these two men are the foremost personalities in Scripture. Of these two individuals, 1 Corinthians 15:47 says, "The first man is from the earth, earthy; the second man is from heaven."

Who are these two who symbolize the essence of masculinity, who serve as the snapshots of manhood? They are Adam and Jesus Christ.

Paul refers to these two men as the "first" and "last" Adams. "So also it is written," writes Paul in 1 Corinthians 15:45, " 'the first man, Adam, became a living soul.' The last Adam [Christ] became a life-giving spirit." Theologian Herman Ridderbos underscores the importance of these two divergent individuals.

> Adam and Christ stand over against each other *as the two great figures* . . . at the entrance of two worlds . . . two creations, the old and the new . . . and in their actions and fate lie the decision for all who belong to them, because *all men are comprehended in them* [emphasis added].[11]

I believe Adam and Jesus Christ represent two different ways of life, leading to two different destinies. In a narrower sense, they also define two different masculinities. Every man needs to know that he will ultimately draw his masculinity from the Adam of Genesis or from Jesus Christ.

The first Adam represents life *separated* from God. His manhood is set on a natural course, a manhood based upon instinct, reaction, and preservation—not revelation. The first Adam represents a failed manhood that seeks to draw life from others; it is manhood devoid of transcendent meaning.

By contrast, the second Adam (Christ) represents *life in union with* God. His manhood is influenced by spiritual direction and based on faith—not flesh. This elevated masculinity, as 1 Corinthians 15:45 says, is life-*giving*, not life-*taking*. It is filled with a meaning and a sense of destiny. But there is more!

When the first Adam is compared with the second Adam, four defining differences appear. I will use these differences to formulate an authentic manhood definition—a definition that is critical today because of the manhood vision it can give. You see, of all things lacking in the lives of men today, the most potent is the answer to the simple question, "What is a man?" These contrasts between Adam and Jesus provide a powerful answer.

MANHOOD PRINCIPLE #1:
A REAL MAN REJECTS PASSIVITY

As you know, boys and men seem to possess a natural aggressiveness to initiate, to explore, and to achieve. When my son Garrett became a teenager, he was literally fuel-injected with testosterone. Garrett's aggressive behavior went into overdrive. He delighted in tripping his younger brother, tackling his sisters, and punching me in the arm. *Pow!* "How ya doin', Dad?"

Though it varies from man to man, this inbred aggressiveness—both physical and psychological—is not a learned behavior; it is innate. It is part of being a man. Yet for Garrett and every other boy, there is no corresponding aggressiveness when it comes to positive social and spiritual action.

For some reason, men of every age become passive when it comes to initiating this action in their homes, with their families, and in their communities. Why? The reason is found in the biblical headwaters of Genesis.

In Genesis 3, the serpent approaches Eve with a tantalizing proposition. He convinces her that the forbidden fruit is actually the path to life. Satan coaxes Eve with the promise that if she takes one bite, she "will be like God" (Genesis 3:5).

The stage is set for Adam to intervene. After all, Adam has been given the responsibility for the garden; the prohibition against eating fruit was spoken to him (Genesis 2:16-17). God has given the first man a *will* to obey ("don't eat the fruit"), a *work* to do ("cultivate the garden"), and a *woman* to love (Eve). These are his explicit responsibilities as a man.

You fully expect Adam to come running with a garden hoe, cut off the serpent's head, and end this heinous approach of evil. But confronted with his social and spiritual responsibilities, Adam becomes, of all things, *passive*.

Have you ever wondered what Adam was doing while Eve was being propositioned? Most people assume that he was absent at the time, communing with nature or tilling the soil. Not true. He was *right there*, watching his wife contemplate moral and spiritual suicide.

Genesis 3:6 tells us so: "When the woman saw that the tree was good for food, and that it was a delight to the eyes, and that the tree was desirable to make one wise, she took from its fruit and ate; and she gave also to her husband with her, and he ate."

Did you hear it? The text says she gave "to her husband *with her.*" As naturally aggressive as Adam was, when the moment of authentic manhood arrived—when he was called upon to act responsibly, take charge spiritually, and protect his woman—Adam just stood there! He went flat. He became passive. He refused to accept the social and spiritual responsibilities entrusted to him by God. Men have been imitating Adam's example ever since. Have you ever wondered why the Bible constantly calls men to love their wives, spiritually instruct their children, and responsibly lead their homes? The reason is because men have a fallen nature that actually bends away from these responsibilities. It comes with maleness. It comes from Adam.

Yale sociologist Stephen B. Clark says flatly, "Men have a natural tendency to avoid social responsibility."[12] Without a vibrant, spiritual solution, this pattern of passivity grows effortlessly. It is now more and more prevalent, and it is breeding death to our culture.

Families cry out for men who will do more than "tune out" when they come home from work. Kids want dads who are involved, dads who provide moral and spiritual direction, dads who are affirming and life-giving. Women want men who will protect them, not use them. Society needs men who will stand for moral absolutes. But we must stop and ask, "Where are these men?" And, "What will become of our families in their absence?"

Paul's answer is almost too painful to bear: "In Adam," he says, "all die" (1 Corinthians 15:22).

But thank God for the second Adam—Jesus Christ! Unlike the first Adam, who stood flat-footed in the face of evil, Jesus Christ *initiated.*

He refused to do nothing when sin encroached upon the created order. He was spiritually and socially aggressive.

In fact, I would argue that we see more manhood in the manger of Jesus than we do in the garden with Adam. Why? Because in the manger we find Jesus, having rejected His divine right as God, initiating toward the world as a man . . . a real man! Listen for the *action words* in Philippians 2:5-8 that describe Christ's redemptive activity. I've highlighted them for you.

> Have this attitude in yourselves which was also in Christ Jesus, who, although He existed in the form of God, did not regard equality with God a thing to be grasped, but *emptied* Himself, *taking the form* of a bond-servant, and being made in the likeness of men. Being found in appearance as a man, He *humbled* Himself by *becoming obedient* to the point of death, even death on a cross.

Real manhood begins with a decision to reject social and spiritual passivity when *nothing* is the more comfortable and *natural* option.

MANHOOD PRINCIPLE #2:
A REAL MAN ACCEPTS RESPONSIBILITY

Like Adam, Jesus Christ was also given three specific responsibilities from His Father. Our Lord was entrusted with a *will* to obey (His Father's), a *work* to do (redeem the lost), and a *"woman"* to love (the church). According to Psalm 40:7-8—a passage that is decidedly Messianic—Jesus Christ accepted these responsibilities with great enthusiasm: "Then I said, 'Behold, I come; in the scroll of the book it is written of me; I delight to do Your will, O my God; Your Law is within my heart.'"

What an incredible contrast with the first Adam, who rejected God's *will,* said no to God's *work,* and refused to love God's *woman.* On all three counts, Jesus Christ did the exact opposite! He accepted His responsibilities, and He did so with joy.

This is illustrated beautifully in John 4:34. After a hard day of ministry, the disciples are hungry and concerned about the health of their master. They bring food to Jesus. He hasn't eaten all day. Nevertheless, Jesus refuses the offering and in the process articulates a principle that is clearly the driving force of His life: "My food is to do the will of Him who sent Me and to accomplish His work."

Jesus allowed these responsibilities to define His life as a man; they gave Him vision and direction. He pursued them energetically and aggressively. From them, He derived great satisfaction.

What causes a man to assume his social and spiritual responsibilities—enthusiastically? If we can assume for the moment a spiritually regenerated heart, I believe sociologist Stephen Clark has a very practical answer.

> Men assume social responsibility most naturally and effectively when (1) it is clear to them that the primary responsibility for the well-being of others rests on them and that others are relying on them, and (2) when they have been trained from an early age by the men in their lives to recognize and assume that responsibility faithfully. [13]

If authentic manhood revolves around three primary responsibilities, then the wise father will train his son to embrace these with enthusiasm: a *will* to obey (God's will as revealed in the Scriptures), a *work* to do (not just in the work of his job, but also the work in his home, church, and community), and a *woman* to love (his wife). If he is going to attain high honor, a Modern-Day Knight must be schooled in these arts, trained from an early age by the mentor in his life: Dad!

Like Tom Minnery's dad. Shortly after his dad underwent an operation for brain cancer, Tom began to feel an urgent need to express to his father the specific impacts his life had made on him. "I knew that was something I should take care of now, knowing his time was limited." He did so in a letter, part of which is replicated here:

> Yes, we all do have to go sometime, but in real measure, we all
> live on in the sons and daughters in whom we invest our lives.
> I wonder if that's where the term "to pass on" comes from.
> People often say individuals have "passed on" when they really
> mean they aren't here anymore. But people really do pass on
> themselves. . . . You have passed on to me and Bill, Don, and
> Greg qualities of devotion to Mom, wise decisions about the
> important matters in life, and that delicate balance between
> concern for your kids and freedom to let them do their own
> things. All of that has worked together very well. Four sons
> with four stable marriages and four solid careers. That's a
> legacy to be proud of in this day. Dad, you have raised us all
> well, and in the process you have given me a *sure road map* for
> my own life. I'm just following you . . .
>
>   Love, Tom [emphasis added][14]

Results like these are no accidents. They are what occur when real men accept their responsibilities.

MANHOOD PRINCIPLE #3:
A REAL MAN LEADS COURAGEOUSLY

Authentic men were designed to lead, not follow. In 1 Corinthians 11:3, the apostle Paul states it this way: "But I want you to understand that Christ is the head of every man, and the man is the head of a woman."

Men were *created* to lead! Adam relinquished his leadership in the garden when he refused to step forward with God's word and lead his wife. This inaction is precisely what many men are doing in our generation—passively yielding to the feelings and emotion of the moment instead of aggressively leading with God's truth. Our homes and communities are in chaos because of it.

Leadership demands that men have the courage to master their passions and bridle themselves with the principle of truth. That is the model Jesus Christ provides. On many occasions, but most notably during His temptation in the wilderness, He demonstrated the leadership of a real man.

After fasting 40 days, Christ was taken by Satan to a high mountain and shown all the kingdoms of the world. Satan then offered our Lord this promise: "All these things will I give You, if You fall down and worship me" (Matthew 4:9). This, of course, compares to Satan's similar pattern of temptation to Eve and to Adam: "Eat and you can have it all!" For 40 days, the Father had led His Son into desolation; in one moment, Satan has shown Him delicious realms of glory. The contrast could not be more poignant, and the contest between passion and principle within Jesus' heart and mind could not have been more powerful.

Yet, this second Adam possessed a courage the first Adam lacked. Like Adam, Christ's emotions cried out for surrender to the seductive "glory" being offered Him. But His will was resolute. His reply energetically resonates with the fiber of authentic manhood: "Then Jesus said to him, 'Begone, Satan! For it is written, "You shall worship the Lord your God, and serve Him only'" (Matthew 4:10, NASB [1977]).

"Begone" is a commanding cry of manly leadership. The Old Testament quotation Jesus then recites from Deuteronomy 6:13 illustrates His embrace of truth. The courage to *lead with truth* rather than surrender to feelings always separates the men from the boys.

MANHOOD PRINCIPLE #4: A REAL MAN EXPECTS THE GREATER REWARD

Manhood is challenging. It can be interpreted as work only: another burden to carry, devoid of joy and satisfaction. The first Adam believed this—and defected for another "glory" being offered him. Clearly, many modern men are defecting for the same reason.

But biblical manhood was never intended to be burdensome. Instead, real manhood was designed by God to be liberating and a means of great *reward.*

Jesus Christ set this example for us as the truly authentic man. Christ embraced His responsibilities—a *will* to obey, a *work* to do, and a *woman* to love—because He anticipated the reward in it all. Listen to Hebrews 12:1-2: "Let us run with endurance the race that is set before us, fixing our eyes on Jesus, the author and perfecter of faith, who for the joy set before Him endured the cross, despising the shame, and has sat down at the right hand of the throne of God."

What kept Jesus in the race? What internal motivation carried Jesus to the cross? *The anticipation of joy!* Great reward. It was the "joy set before Him" that allowed Christ to finish strong. Every man needs to have this same perspective if he is to succeed.

Moses was certainly energized by this principle. "By faith Moses, when he had grown up, refused to be called the son of Pharaoh's daughter, choosing rather to endure ill-treatment with the people of God than to enjoy the passing pleasures of sin . . . for he was looking to *the reward"* (Hebrews 11:24-26, emphasis added).

The great lawgiver of Israel pursued authentic manhood because it promised great reward.

If you think the call to manhood is a call merely to heavy responsibility and dutiful sacrifice, then you've completely missed the example of the second Adam. Yes, real manhood is at times rigorous; it demands courage and requires sacrifice. Nevertheless, it is primarily a *call to life!*

> I came that they may have life, and might have it abundantly. (John 10:10)

> But just as it is written, "Things which eye has not seen and ear has not heard, and which have not entered the heart of man, all that God has prepared for those who love Him." (1 Corinthians 2:9)

> For bodily discipline is only of little profit, but godliness is profitable for all things, since it holds promise for the present life and also for the life to come. (1 Timothy 4:8)

> Godliness actually is a means of great gain. (1 Timothy 6:6)

Men, I submit to you that my own quest for authentic manhood— to whatever degree I have achieved it—has been accompanied by great gains and rewards. By the grace of God I have been rewarded with . . .

- an honorable name.
- a wife who looks at me with respect and admiration. Yes, at times it has been hard to live for her, but I have fought to be faithful to her. Today I enjoy her respect and affirmation.
- four well-adjusted, responsible children who contribute to others and to the kingdom of God.
- the respect of other men in the community.
- innumerable experiences of God's blessings.
- a growing satisfaction about my life.

There is no way I could have known all that on the front end or anticipated all the wonderful events in store for me as I've pursued real manhood in Jesus Christ. On the other hand, I didn't accept my calling for nothing! King David and I are in solid agreement on this point. He said it this way in Psalm 27:13: "I would have despaired unless I had believed that I would see the goodness of the Lord."

No one does anything for nothing. I believed from the start that the way of Christ is *life* (John 14:6). I believed all along that the manhood found in Him would be fulfilling and rewarding . . . and I was right. The manhood of Christ is a manhood of *reward.*

THE CORNERSTONES

So there you have it—four distinguishing differences between the first Adam and the second; the four cornerstones of a foundation that define for us the essence of authentic manhood. What is a real man? From the lives of Adam and Jesus comes the following powerful reply. A real man is one who:

- rejects passivity
- accepts responsibility

• leads courageously

• expects the greater reward . . . God's reward.

This manhood vision desperately needs to be proclaimed throughout our society. It is a vision that makes its greatest impact when transmitted from fathers to their Modern-Day Knights.

When my son Garrett was 13, he and his friends met with our youth pastor for their weekly discipleship group. Garrett's pastor, Mark DeYmaz, thought it would be beneficial to talk about manhood. Mark asked the guys if they knew what it meant to be a man.

Without hesitation, Garrett replied, "I do."

"Tell us the answer," said Mark, a bit surprised by Garrett's decisiveness.

"A man," he promptly announced, "is someone who rejects passivity, accepts responsibility, leads courageously, and expects a greater reward."

Somewhat dumbfounded, Mark asked, "Where did you learn that, Garrett?"

"From my dad."

And that's the way it ought to be!

Key Moves for Presenting a Manhood Vision to a Son

- First and foremost, settle upon a manhood definition that you and your son can pursue together. You cannot call your son to a vision you cannot define. And remember, the deeper your commitment to personally pursue this vision yourself, the better for your son. It must be real to you in order to be real to him.

- Teach this definition of manhood to your son at puberty. Have him memorize it as the ideal to which you will point his—and your own—life. Use it as a teaching tool in his everyday life in the spirit of Deuteronomy 6:6-7.

- If you have a preteen son (age 6-12), expand your fatherhood vision by joining with other dads and going through my *Raising a Modern-Day Knight Video Adventure Series*. Go to www.RMDK.com for more information.

- Team up with some dads and create a manhood weekend for your sons. This is especially powerful for boys 17 and older. Include fun and intimate discussions on what it means to be a man. End the weekend with a challenge to your sons to pursue real manhood, and then "spike it" with a ceremony of commitment.

- Conduct several specific manhood ceremonies for your son in his march to manhood. (Chapters 7-10 offer a number of helpful ways to create these.)

- Host a father-son Bible study on "The Pursuit of Authentic Manhood." One way to do this is using my six-part *Becoming a Man* video study for dads with teenage sons. Go to www.mensfraternity.com for more information.

CHAPTER 5

A CODE
OF CONDUCT

More than a code of manners in war and love,
Chivalry was a moral system,
governing the whole of noble life.
—BARBARA W. TUCHMAN, *A DISTANT MIRROR*

I remember well that painful day when the piercing words of my sixth grade teacher came crashing down upon me. She had just caught me cheating on her science exam.

"Robert," she said as I awaited sentencing, "you are what you are when no one is looking."

With that penetrating shot to the heart, she let me go free. Well, sort of.

Her words went with me. They marked me for life. I've heard

those words dozens of times, replayed in the secrecy of my soul, warning me of what moral compromise really means. They have inspired me to reach higher.

As a dad, you will have these same life-marking moral opportunities with your son from time to time.

In his story appropriately titled "Catch of a Lifetime," James P. Lenfestey describes one such defining moment. He tells of an 11-year-old boy eagerly anticipating the opening of bass season. At 10:00 on the night before the season opened, the boy practiced casting with his dad from the dock of his family cabin set on a New Hampshire lake. Suddenly, his pole doubled over. He had hooked something . . . something heavy.

The excitement that followed was absolutely glorious, but nothing compared to the great fish that was lifted from the dark water minutes later. It was the largest bass the boy or his father had ever seen.

The father lit a match and looked at his watch. Then he made this stinging pronouncement: "You'll have to put it back, son."

Bass season was two hours away. Just two hours! No one was in sight, so who would know the difference? And yet, the boy's father insisted.

The incident occurred more than 40 years ago. Never again would the boy catch such a magnificent fish. But what he did catch that day was something much better: a lesson in moral character.

For, as his father taught him, ethics are simple matters of right and wrong. It is only the practice of ethics that is difficult. Do we do right when no one is looking? Do we refuse to cut corners . . . ? We would if we were taught to put the fish back when we were young. For we would have learned the truth.

> The decision to do right . . . is a story we will proudly tell our
> friends and our grandchildren. Not about how we had a
> chance to beat the system and took it, but about how we did
> the right thing and were forever strengthened.[1]

These last two words summarize the effect of principled, moral instruction by a father: When a dad imparts a code of conduct, when he establishes boundaries and reinforces truth, a son is *forever strengthened.* Learned at an early age, ethical standards become a beacon in the midst of a darkened society, a lighthouse that steers us away from the rugged coastline of moral destruction. "The integrity of the upright will guide them," asserts the writer of Proverbs, "but the crookedness of the treacherous will destroy them" (11:3).

OUR CHANGING MORAL CLIMATE

Every son needs a Code of Conduct. This "weapon of the spirit" becomes even more imperative when you consider the immoral character of modern society. Gone are the days when infractions like talking out of turn, chewing gum, and running in the halls were considered major problems in our schools. Today the challenges require on-site police officers, metal detectors, and grief counselors.

There was a time when family values were reinforced by the culture, but that time is long past. William Kilpatrick writes:

> Parents cannot, as they once did, rely on the culture to rein-
> force home values. In fact, they can expect that many of the
> cultural forces influencing their children will be actively under-
> mining those values.[2]

A Knight's Code of Conduct

Once again, we can learn a thing or two from our medieval counter-parts. From an early age, the page and then the squire apprenticed under men with social and moral ideals; they were personally trained in ethical standards that gave form and substance to life despite the morally hostile culture.

First, a knight was expected to be *loyal.* In the words of Barbara Tuchman, "Loyalty, meaning the pledged word, was chivalry's ful-crum. . . . A knight who broke his oath was charged with 'treason' for betraying the order of knighthood."[3]

Next, the knight was expected to *conduct himself like a champion.* Every aspect of his behavior—whether in combat or in social set-tings—was to exude courage and valor. Third, the knight was charged to *win the love of women*: to be romantic and chivalrous. And fourth, the medieval knight was required to practice generosity, or *largess.* Says Georges Duby, "The knight owes it to himself to keep nothing in his hands. All that comes to him he gives away."[4]

The code exerted tremendous influence in society because, as Frances Gies points out, "Many men in the Middle Ages embraced [the ideals] and tried to live by them: honor, unselfish service, dedica-tion to justice, and protest against war's brutalities."[5]

The Modern-Day Knight, like his medieval counterpart, must be trained in a Code of Conduct. According to Scripture, every son— from an early age—must be schooled in three critical areas I men-tioned in the previous chapter:

A will to obey (God's will)
A work to do (according to his own unique design)
A woman to love

Lacking these elements, a son will flounder in adulthood; he will wrestle with feelings of inadequacy, incompetence, and restlessness. But armed with them, a son becomes equipped to succeed in his relationship with God, in his community and church, and in his marriage.

A WILL TO OBEY

King Solomon, like most contemporary existentialists, lived his life as if the past were irrelevant and the future uncertain. He drank, collected women, gathered possessions, and cultivated knowledge, only to discover in the end that these pursuits were futile.

Near the end of his life, filled with remorse and regret, Solomon articulated a principle that speaks to us down through the ages. The words are simple, but their meaning and application are profound. In Ecclesiastes 12:1, he writes: "Remember also your Creator in the days of your youth."

It was a truth he himself had forgotten somewhere along the way. And why is this admonition so important? Solomon answers this question in the last two verses of the same chapter:

> The conclusion, when all has been heard, is: fear God and
> keep His commandments, because this applies to every person.
> For God will bring every act to judgment, everything which is
> hidden, whether it is good or evil. (Ecclesiastes 12:13-14)

Like Solomon, modern man has also forgotten the wisdom of a will greater than his own. The outcome is what Dr. Richard Halverson, former chaplain of the United States Senate, called "destination sickness":

. . . the syndrome of the man who has arrived and discovered he is nowhere. He has achieved his goals and finds they are not what he had anticipated. He suffers the disillusionments of promises that petered out—the payoff with the kickback! He has all the things money can buy and finds decreasing satisfaction in all he has. . . .

He's the man who has become a whale of a success downtown and a pathetic failure at home. He's the big shot with the boys in the office and a big phony with the boys at home. He's the status symbol in society and a fake with the family. "Destination Sickness"—the illness peculiar to a culture that is affluent and godless.[6]

The first—and arguably the most important—lesson a young man must learn is that life is inherently *moral.* There is a divine will to obey. Every son needs to know that there is an all-powerful (Genesis 18:14), all-seeing (Psalm 139:1-4), holy (1 Peter 1:14-16) God who rewards good and punishes evil. He must be taught that absolute values exist; that the commandments of God are liberating, not restrictive (John 8:31-32).

Every young man needs a comprehensive view of life that begins with this fundamental proposition: *True satisfaction in life is directly proportionate to one's obedience to God.* In this context, moral boundaries take on a whole new perspective: They become *benefits,* not *burdens.*

TEN BIBLICAL IDEAS

The handbook for Modern-Day Knights is the Bible. Following are 10 biblical ideals a wise father can impart to his son. These ideals constitute the chain links in the Code of Conduct.

Loyalty

"For I delight in loyalty rather than sacrifice, and in the knowledge of God rather than burnt offerings" (Hosea 6:6).

Servant-leadership

"Whoever wishes to become great among you shall be your servant, and whoever wishes to be first among you shall be your slave" (Matthew 20:26-27).

Kindness

"What is desirable in a man is his kindness" (Proverbs 19:22).

Humility

"Do nothing from selfishness or empty conceit, but with humility of mind regard one another as more important than yourselves" (Philippians 2:3).

Purity

"Let no one look down on your youthfulness, but rather in speech, conduct, love, faith and purity, show yourself an example of those who believe" (1 Timothy 4:12).

Honesty

"Therefore, laying aside falsehood, speak truth each one of you with his neighbor, for we are members of one another" (Ephesians 4:25).

Self-discipline

"Have nothing to do with worldly fables. . . . On the other hand, discipline yourself for the purpose of godliness; for bodily discipline is only of little profit, but godliness is profitable for all things, since it holds promise for the present life and also for the life to come" (1 Timothy 4:7-8).

Excellence

"Do you not know that those who run in a race all run, but only one receives the prize? Run in such a way that you may win" (1 Corinthians 9:24).

Integrity

"He who walks in integrity walks securely, but he who perverts his ways will be found out" (Proverbs 10:9).

Perseverance

"Let us not lose heart in doing good, for in due time we will reap if we do not grow weary" (Galatians 6:9).

FOUR KEYS TO EFFECTIVE TRAINING

How does a father train his "page" to obey God's will, to embrace these ideals as his very own? I believe there are four primary ways:

1. A father must *set a godly example.* Bryce Jessup is president of San Jose Christian College in California. He and his wife, Jo, have raised three children; one daughter is married to a missionary, the other daughter is married to a pastor, and the son is a pastor. Some time ago, Bryce's son, Jimmy, was required to write a college paper on the subject "Why I am the way I am." It contained this paragraph:

My mother is a fantastic lady who always encouraged me in the Word, yet my father is the reason I devoted my life to the ministry. I watched my father pretty closely as I was growing up. Like most young boys, I wanted to be just like Dad. I was one of the lucky ones, though, in that I had a dad worth patterning my life after. To me, he is a great man—not because of his success in ministry, but because of his ability to keep Christ as the focus in all that he does. At work, at home, and on vacation, I never saw him set Christ aside. I am the way I am because I see in him a life that is worth trying to repeat.

Sons watch their father's example—whether they are godly or not.

2. A father trains his page to obey God's will by *teaching spiritual truth.* This training may take the form of a quiet time between father and son, or a regularly scheduled family devotion. According to Deuteronomy 6:6-7, the best training occurs in the classroom of life. Addressing fathers, Moses says:

These words, which I am commanding you today, shall be on your heart. You shall teach them diligently to your sons and shall talk of them when you sit in your house and when you walk by the way and when you lie down and when you rise up.

We often view spiritual training as an *event*: God expands it to include a *lifestyle!* The father who has committed himself to these ideals and has placed them upon his own heart is continually looking for opportunities to teach them to his son.

As Moses says, these teachable moments can occur "when you sit in your house." Around the dinner table. In the living room. Spiritual instruction can also occur "when you walk by the way." At the park. At the mall. On the ball field. When you are fishing together. Or "when you lie down." At bedtime. Or "when you rise up." At the breakfast table.

Teaching spiritual truth in the classroom of life is highly memorable. The young man in the fishing story never forgot the lesson his father taught him because it immediately applied to his life. This kind of instruction carries weight and leaves a boy *forever strengthened.*

3. A father trains his son to obey biblical truth by *sharing stories.* Imagine a young boy in medieval society sitting beside a fire at night while his father tells him stories about knights. The son falls asleep dreaming about glory and honor. To repeat the words of Frances Gies, these stories "fixed the self-image of the knight. . . . [They] helped to define standards for knightly behavior."[7]

Good stories have the same effect in our day. Children are mesmerized by vivid accounts of courage and bravery and sacrifice—real or fictional. The wise dad illustrates manhood ideals by telling or reading stories to his boy. The anthologies by William Bennett (*The Book of Virtues* and *The Children's Book of Virtues*) are great places to start.

4. A father reinforces the will to obey through *affirmation, attention,* and *discipline.* As I have talked to many men about their dads over the years, one thing continually surfaces: *Most men say their fathers' approach to right and wrong was primarily to punish and belittle them for what they did wrong, not to praise or encourage them for what they did right.* Discipline was rarely positive. More often it was:

"You screwed up!"

"Why can't you make better grades?"

"You're grounded for a month!"

"Clean up your room!"

"You're always late!"

It's a familiar pattern, and one that's hard to change. Sons receive their dads' harshness (usually at the end of a long workday), but rarely their patient instruction, focused attention, or consistent affirmation.

When a son does something *right,* the wise father praises his character as well as behavior; when he does something *wrong,* the wise father takes time to correct and instruct first, disciplining only as a last resort.

A godly example, teachable moments, inspiring stories, positive affirmation—these are a dad's greatest assets in helping his young knight discover a will to obey.

A WORK TO DO

Life is bigger than a job. That's a good thing, too, because, according to Genesis 3, occupational labor is a source of pain and frustration. You will recall that, following Adam's disobedience in the garden, God said: "Cursed is the ground because of you; in toil you will eat of it all the days of your life. Both thorns and thistles it shall grow for you; and you shall eat the plants of the field; by the sweat of your face you will eat bread" (verses 17-19).

For thousands of years men have tried to extract ultimate meaning and significance from their jobs. Many of us seek fulfillment in our careers, thinking the marketplace will satisfy our deepest yearnings. But life was never designed this way. King Solomon summarized the frustration many of us feel with respect to our jobs when he wrote: "What does a man get in all his labor and in his striving with which he labors under the sun? Because all his days his task is painful and grievous; even at night his mind does not rest. This too is vanity" (Ecclesiastes 2:22-23).

Does this mean we are condemned to a life of futile employment? Absolutely not! In the very next sentence, Solomon writes: "There is nothing better for a man than to eat and drink and tell himself that his labor is good. This also I have seen that it is from the hand of God" (verse 24). And then he adds, "For who can eat and who can have enjoyment without Him?" (verse 25)

Here's Solomon's logic: Labor is painful and frustrating, but what redeems and enriches it is the laborer's relationship to God.

God created each of us to do a twofold work. The first is our chosen profession. Every man and every son has been designed with unique gifts and abilities. Some of us are architects; others are athletes or lawyers or pastors. As many of us have learned by experience, fulfillment at work increases when we labor in an area of strength, not weakness.

Learning Your Child's Inner Design

For this reason, it is imperative that we help our sons identify their gifts at an early age, so they can maximize their abilities. Proverbs 22:6 gives us some insight into this important area: "Train up a child in the way he should go, even when he is old he will not depart from it." In his outstanding book *Different Children, Different Needs*, Charles F. Boyd makes the following observation:

> The phrase "in the way he should go" does not refer to some prescribed path that every person should follow. In the Hebrew language, the phrase is better rendered, "according to his way." And the Hebrew word for "way" is *derek*, which literally means "bent" and refers to a unique inner design or direction.[8]

Unfortunately, some dads miss this vital truth. One man wrote me the following letter:

My dad tried to teach me how to play baseball when I was a kid, but I was never interested in sports. This made him real mad. I could feel his constant displeasure over this. I later got real interested in electronics, but he wasn't any more interested in that than I was in baseball. At my request, he would take me to an electronics store on Saturday and drop me off for a few hours, but that's about as far as our interaction went.

Instead of forcing a child to pursue the father's path, the wise dad helps his son pursue the *son's* particular bent, his area of giftedness. The father nurtures and encourages his child's gifts and abilities, exposes him to a variety of opportunities while he is young, and then focuses his interests as he grows older.

The second aspect of "a work to do" relates to more than a chosen profession; it encompasses a son's *spiritual* giftedness. God has designed men to contribute to the *whole* community, specifically to the church and kingdom work. Says 1 Peter 4:10, "As each one has received a special gift, employ it in serving one another as good stewards of the manifold grace of God."

Over the last few years, our church has emphasized the importance of giftedness through a "Discover Your Design" course taught by one of our pastors. In that class, church members have the opportunity to explore their unique personalities and abilities. Afterward, a follow-up "Dream Class" allows them, with the help of others, to explore ways to use these special gifts for Christ.

One man, who by his own admission was "bored with church" and himself, came alive when he found he could use his media and marketing gifts to craft television commercials for the church that would impact the surrounding community. The results have been award-winning advertising and a new satisfaction with life.

Life is more than a job. Sons need to hear this from a dad. They need to see this in his life. Nothing satisfies the human heart as fully as service for the kingdom—in one's area of giftedness.

So, Dad . . . do you know your son's unique bent? Have you helped him envision how his gifts could be utilized in a vocation and in God's kingdom? Your "page" needs this kind of mentoring if he is to become a Modern-Day Knight.

A WOMAN TO LOVE

This third element of our Code of Conduct prepares a son to succeed in marriage. It addresses the most important earthly relationship he will have throughout the course of his life.

The chivalric literature of medieval times revered the primacy of male-female relationships. The knight was instructed to treat women with respect and honor. For example, when Percival leaves home in the story of King Arthur, his mother says, "You will soon be a knight, my son. . . . If you encounter, near or far, a lady in need of help, or any damsel in distress, be ready to aid her if she asks you to, for all honor lies in such deeds. When a man fails to honor ladies, his own honor must be dead."[9]

Similarly, our sons must be instructed to love, lead, and honor the opposite sex. If, God willing, your son marries one day, his wife will play a central role in his life. The Lord Himself recognized the masculine hunger for female companionship when He said, "It is not good for the man to be alone" (Genesis 2:18).

Boys become men, and most men get married. But the quality of a marital relationship often depends upon a father's tutelage (or lack thereof) earlier in life. According to Scripture, one of a man's chief responsibilities is to care for the woman in his life. Ephesians 5:25-30 outlines the way:

> Husbands, love your wives, just as Christ also loved the church and gave Himself up for her, so that He might sanctify her, having cleansed her by the washing of water with the word, that He might present to Himself the church in all her glory, having no spot or wrinkle or any such thing; but that she would be holy and blameless. So husbands ought also to love their own wives as their own bodies. He who loves his own wife loves himself; for no one ever hated his own flesh, but nourishes and cherishes it, just as Christ also does the church, because we are members of His body.

Is it overstating the obvious to say that this is one of the most neglected passages in the whole Bible? Oh, we may hear Ephesians 5 quoted at weddings, but the application of those truths is sorely absent in our society. One of the loudest complaints we hear today is from women who are tired of being abused and mistreated by their husbands.

Examples of domestic abuse have saturated the media. In a powerful music video by Martina McBride entitled "Independence Day," images of liberty and freedom were continually contrasted with a home filled with domestic violence. In one sequence, we caught a glimpse of a wife who had been battered by her husband. Later on, a little girl left the house to attend a July 4 parade while her mother was being pummeled by her dad. When the little girl returned home after the parade, the house was on fire with the dad inside. The not-so-subtle message was, *We're not gonna take it anymore!*

An increasing number of young men are growing up without any model or teaching on how to love women. In one of my Men's Fraternity meetings, I discussed the biblical imperative of caring for women. After the meeting, two young men approached me; one was married, the other single. Both said they had *never been told* it was their responsibility to care for women and provide for them. Never.

Such comments should come as no surprise to us, in light of the manhood vacuum of today. To add insult to injury, contemporary feminism has prided itself in turning honorable acts of chivalry into dishonorable acts of chauvinism. Men *care* for women? No way!

But according to Ephesians 5, it *is* the responsibility of men to care for women. I recognize this discussion of love for a woman requires a whole book, and many fine ones have already been written on the subject. But let the bottom line be stated clearly right here: *Men are called by God to love, lead, and honor their wives.* This is the crown jewel in the Code of Conduct, an heirloom that must be transmitted from father to son.

A will to obey . . .

A work to do . . .

A woman to love.

By these three components in our Code of Conduct, a son is *forever strengthened.* Tragically, the first man—Adam—relinquished each of these responsibilities. But the second Adam—Christ—embraced them passionately. So, too, will Modern-Day Knights!

Key Moves for Presenting a Code of Conduct to a Son

- First and foremost, establish a written code of conduct that you want your son to embrace before leaving home. If you need help, see my book *Real Family Values* (Multnomah, 2000). Be sure that whatever code of conduct you settle on is one you are committed to pursuing yourself. Remember, you will leave in your sons what you have lived out at home.

- Discern your child's design and then encourage the support and development of that natural gifting. Don't try to make him something he's not. Charles Boyd's book *Different Children, Different Needs,* published by Multnomah Press, is extremely helpful in this regard.

- Read books to your boy that carry strong moral messages. Bible stories are foundational. If you read to your son early and make it fun, he will read for a lifetime.

- Teach your teenage son about relating to women, both socially and sexually. Perhaps other dads will join you with their sons for a series of group discussions on this essential subject. I would suggest you read my book *Rocking the Roles,* published by NavPress, as a foundation to this study. There are, however, a number of excellent resources available that could serve as the focus of your discussion. It is critically important that boys be told about their role and responsibilities in regard to young women now and in a future marriage relationship.

- Teach your son generosity. Show him what you give to the church monthly. Explain why you do this. Show him what you give to charities. Take him with you on church and community service projects, mission trips, and the like. Teach him that he, like you, should tithe a portion of his time, money, and talents to others.

- Protect your son in his preteen years from the negative influence of television and movies. As an adolescent, set high standards for him and yourself concerning media influences—and explain why! The more you model this for him, the more he will follow your lead.
- Establish a work ethic in your son by tying his allowance to specific chores around the house and performance at school. During his teenage years, require your son to find some kind of summer job.

CHAPTER 6

A Transcendent Cause

The happiest man is he who is able to
integrate the end of his life with its beginning.
—GOETHE

The summer sun beat down upon the blue Pacific. A lone skiff, ferrying a handful of old men, glided slowly across the surface of the water and made its way toward the beach. Waves lapped against the bow; a gentle breeze, refreshing and seductive, softened the searing afternoon heat.

Tom Quinn, 68, was the first to recognize the tranquil beauty of this tropical paradise. "I'm in awe. I'm really in awe," he said. "I feel like crying. It's so beautiful now. It should have been beautiful then." Under a cloudless sky, the skiff nestled onto the sandy white beach.

One by one, the old men stepped gingerly from the boat. Some of them wept. A few stood motionless, surveying the landscape that had become entombed in their collective consciousness. No one spoke. For each of the retired warriors, the tranquility was shattered by memories from the past life: machine gun fire, the cries of wounded comrades, stifling heat, and the stench of death.

For Tom Quinn and his companions, the nightmare had come full circle. After 50 years of soul-searching, they had returned to the scene of one of the bloodiest battles of World War II: the island of Peleliu. These veterans carried on their bodies the scars of war and nursed in their hearts the wounds of the spirit. They were haunted by the ferocity of the battle and the death of friends. But to a man, the deepest scar—the most painful wound—was the knowledge that they had fought a battle that was completely unnecessary.

It wasn't supposed to be that way.

Back in 1944, General Douglas MacArthur designed a strategy to reclaim the Philippines and attack Japan. This entailed conquering a succession of islands between Hawaii and the Philippines, building runways, and then dropping bombs on Japanese strongholds. When 9,000 American troops stormed ashore on Peleliu in September 1944, they believed their thrust was crucial to victory in the Pacific. It wasn't.

While the Americans slugged it out with 12,000 well-fortified Japanese soldiers, the war passed them by; other GIs were already landing just south of the Philippines with little resistance.

More than 8,500 Americans were killed or wounded in the struggle for Peleliu. In terms of death per square mile, it was the bloodiest battle of World War II. But it was all for nothing. And as an NBC *Dateline* reporter watched Tom Quinn and his comrades tour the battlefield 50 years later, he remarked, "The veterans of Peleliu have a very hard time with the idea that history has judged their sacrifice irrelevant."[1]

WHAT'S THE POINT?

Nothing grates on a man's spirit quite like *irrelevance.* The knowledge that our best efforts and heroic deeds were meaningless is a bitter pill to swallow. "I have been everything," moaned the Roman emperor Septimus, "and it is worth nothing."[2] At the height of his success, Napoleon wrote to his brother Joseph, "I am tired of glory at twenty-nine; it has lost its charm; and there is nothing left for me but complete egotism."[3]

In a much larger sense, the battle for Peleliu is symbolic of modern man's daily experience. The typical young male in our society invests his time and energy in a bevy of self-centered activities—his career, his pleasures, his possessions—all the while believing they will matter beyond the moment. But sometime later in life, often in the late 30s or early 40s, he discovers a sobering reality: He's won the battle but lost the war. The glory of material prosperity and corporate success loses its charm, and he feels nothing but a gnawing question of "What else is there?"

Abd-al-Rahman III, notable caliph of Spain from A.D. 912 to 961, exposed the folly of loving vocational success and personal affluence when he said this before his death:

I have now reigned above fifty years in victory or peace. . . .
Riches and honor, powers and pleasures have waited on my
call; nor does any earthly blessing appear to have been wanting
to my felicity. In this situation I have diligently numbered the

days of pure and genuine happiness which have fallen to my
lot. They amount to fourteen. O man! place not thy confidence in this present world.[4]

This "conventional vision of manhood," as I call it, has five celebrated characteristics. First, and perhaps most importantly, *it paints a
one-dimensional picture, equating manhood with a "position."* When
you ask a man, "Who are you?" the conventional man replies, "I'm a
carpenter," or "I'm an attorney." The emphasis is upon what a man
does, not who he *is.*

Second, because a man's identity arises from his work, *his value is
earned; therefore, he becomes highly competitive.* Credibility comes by
accomplishing, by winning. The conventional man's objective is to
out-*think,* out-*work,* out-*play,* and out-*earn* the other guy.

Third, in this vision of manhood, *success is the goal—often at the
expense of one's marriage, one's children, and meaningful, close relationships.*

Fourth, *the reward of conventional manhood is power, chiefly in the
marketplace.* By reaching a level of success, a man commands the
respect and attention of those around him, with a power that can be
intoxicating if he is not careful.

And finally, *if a man becomes successful in this plan, he enjoys personal wealth and affluence.* He is admired by the world and privileged
to do what others can't, but it rarely satisfies. Why? Listen to the words
of one of the world's foremost conventional men, King Solomon:

I enlarged my works: I built houses for myself, I planted vine-
yards for myself; I made gardens and parks for myself and I
planted in them all kinds of fruit trees; I made ponds of water
for myself from which to irrigate a forest of growing trees. I
bought male and female slaves and I had homeborn slaves.

Also I possessed flocks and herds larger than all who preceded
me in Jerusalem. Also, I collected for myself silver and gold
and the treasure of kings and provinces. I provided for myself
male and female singers and the pleasures of men—many concubines. Then I became great and increased more than all who
preceded me in Jerusalem. My wisdom also stood by me. And
all that my eyes desired I did not refuse them. I did not with-
hold my heart from any pleasure, for my heart was pleased
because of all my labor and this was my reward for all my
labor. Thus I considered all my activities which my hands had
done and the labor which I had exerted, and behold all was
vanity and striving after wind and there was no profit under
the sun. (Ecclesiastes 2:4-11)

The problem with this conventional model of manhood is not
that it is wrong, but that it is *incomplete.* As a part of life, there is nothing wrong with pursuing a career and success and all the trappings
(minus the concubines!) that go with it. The problem is in thinking
this is *all of life* when, in fact, it is only a part.

Something critical is missing! It is the one component that puri-
fies our efforts, lends dignity to our lives, and ensures satisfaction
beyond the moment. In three simple but profound words, what is
missing is *a transcendent cause.*

SOMETHING BEYOND OURSELVES

What is a transcendent cause? It is a mission that lifts us beyond ourselves, a passion that stirs us to a self-sacrifice and causes us to contribute to the larger community. A transcendent cause is not something
we do *in addition to* everything else; instead, *it is the one factor that*

motivates everything else we do. Put in the simplest terms, we want our lives to count for something important.

In her book *Pathfinders,* Gail Sheehy lists what she calls "The Ten Hallmarks of Well-being." Not surprisingly, at the top of her list is the conviction that one's life must possess "meaning and direction." She writes: "People of high well-being find meaning in an involvement with something *beyond themselves:* a work, an idea, other people, a social objective" [emphasis added].[5]

True satisfaction in life is impossible apart from a transcendent cause. Listen to the words of sociologist Ernest Becker:

> Man will lay down his life for his country, his society, his family. He will choose to throw himself on a grenade to save his comrades; he is capable of the highest generosity and self-sacrifice. But he has to feel and believe that what he is doing is truly heroic, timeless, and supremely meaningful.[6]

What are the characteristics of a transcendent cause? Becker identifies three. (As I note each one, you'll discover that the bulk of our pursuits—career, pleasure, possessions—fail to pass the test.)

- A transcendent cause must be *truly heroic,* a noble endeavor calling forth bravery and sacrifice.
- A transcendent cause must be *timeless.* It contains significance beyond the moment.
- A transcendent cause must be *supremely meaningful.* It pulsates with meaning.

Sadly, many of our youth know little or nothing about any cause other than themselves. Parents have failed—and are failing—to impart a vision that is truly heroic, timeless, and supremely meaningful. The consequences of this omission cannot be understated.

William Damon, professor of education at Brown University, makes this potent observation:

> When we teach children to concern themselves first and foremost with their own sense of self, we not only encourage self-centeredness but also fail to present a more inspiring and developmentally constructive alternative: that they should concern themselves about things *beyond* the self and *above* the self. We fail, that is, to convey to them a sense that there are other important things in life beyond their own individual circumstances and feelings.[7]

How does this apply to fathers with sons looking to them for leadership? Often in the following ways:

- We invest our sons with marketplace *competence,* but not moral *conviction.*
- We help our sons to become socially *successful,* but not spiritually *significant.*
- We give our sons *good* things, but not the *best* things.

When this happens, our sons will in time experience the same woundedness, wastedness, and betrayal of those sad soldiers of Peleliu.

The only antidote to the futility of life is a transcendent cause. Until a son discovers and commits himself to a cause that is *truly heroic, timeless,* and *supremely meaningful,* no amount of pleasure or success is going to satisfy his heart. King Solomon ultimately came to this same, painful conclusion and left us a record in his timeless book of wisdom. In this verse he also points us in the right direction: "Remember also your Creator in the days of your youth, before the evil days come and the years draw near when you will say, 'I have no delight in them'" (Ecclesiastes 12:1).

A Tortured Journey

Let me illustrate this through a story of a close friend of mine.

When Bill Smith boarded the small American Airlines prop-jet from Dallas to Little Rock, he was weary. It was late in the afternoon, and by his own admission he felt "grubby." The 55-year-old investment counselor plopped into a window seat, hoping no one would sit next to him.

But God had other plans. Just when it looked as if Bill's wish might come true, a six-foot-three-inch stranger settled into the aisle seat. The flight attendant secured the door, and the plane taxied down the runway. As much as Bill wanted to sit quietly and reflect during his trip, he felt compelled to say something to his neighbor. "After all," Bill told me later, "he was too close to ignore."

Bill broke the silence. "Where are you going?" he asked.

"To Pine Bluff," the man replied. That one question let loose a flood of information. The stranger, whose name was Jim, went on to tell Bill that he did consulting work for the government and was traveling to visit a military arsenal. He claimed he was responsible for a third of his company's revenues. He told Bill he hated to travel but couldn't get off the road. He talked about college and the investment he'd made to secure an education. And he mentioned the fact that he'd been married for a year and a half and had inherited a 13-year-old stepson in the process.

Between snippets of conversation, Bill glanced at Jim. The man baring his soul was in his early 30s; he had dark features and dark, piercing eyes. But to Bill Smith, Jim's most noticeable characteristic was his demeanor. He was energetic, but there was a tone of sadness in his voice.

Bill quickly realized he was talking with a younger version of his former self.

Like his neighbor, Bill Smith knew a thing or two about success—and disappointment.

In his younger days, Bill had three key goals. First, he had wanted to make a lot of money. As the director of the Capital Management Division at Stephens, Inc., Bill had accomplished this first goal in abundance. He had traded stocks and commodities for clients in Europe, Asia, and the United States, and earned large commissions. Second, Bill had wanted to meet powerful, influential people. He had achieved this as well, numbering then-Governor Bill Clinton among his many clients. His last goal was to travel all over the world. He had done so many times.

But with all of his worldly success, Bill couldn't fill the hole in his heart. It cried out for satisfaction. So the man with everything began to seek fulfillment in other ways: He drank, he partied, he dabbled in New Age and Eastern religions. Nevertheless, the emptiness remained.

At the age of 47, in a hotel room in Salt Lake City, Bill Smith discovered something that changed his life forever. While waiting for his wife, Cydney, to dress for dinner, Bill reached nonchalantly into a drawer and opened a Bible. He turned to the Gospel of John and read words that stirred his heart: "But as many as received Him, to them He gave the right to become children of God, even to those who believe in His name, who were born, not of blood nor of the will of the flesh nor of the will of man, but of God" (John 1:12-13).

Something about these verses ignited a fire in Bill Smith. He decided that once he returned to Little Rock he would purchase a Bible and read some more. He did. Bill started reading the Scriptures for 20 minutes a day, taking notes along the way. He recorded his findings in a journal.

Five months into his study, an amazing thing occurred. "I got the sense," he says, "that Jesus Christ was meeting with me personally. His presence demanded my respect. I couldn't shake it. In the process, I came to a sobering conclusion. I realized that Jesus Christ was alive. And if He's alive, then He must be God."

Bill Smith discovered his transcendent cause.

Little changes soon became evident in the way Bill related to other people. He used to be so driven that he hated interruptions at work; he instructed his assistants not to put through any phone calls or allow anyone into his presence unless they could "help him make money." But the new Bill found himself taking time for others. Interruptions became divine appointments. He asked intruders how they were doing and listened intently for an answer.

As months passed and Jesus Christ became an increasingly intimate friend, Bill Smith realized that the hole in his heart was gone; it had been filled by the God of the universe.

Working for a King

In time Jim finished talking about himself and asked, "What do you do?"

"Well," replied Bill, "I do a number of things, but the most exciting thing I do is work for a King."

"A king?" Jim exclaimed. His face was flushed with curiosity.

"Yes, a King," said Bill.

"From the Middle East?"

"As a matter of fact, He is. He's very wealthy and very powerful."

"Which one is it?"

"Oh," replied Bill, "this King is quite mysterious."

Jim guessed—incorrectly—a few Middle Eastern potentates.

"What do you do for this king?" he asked.

Bill responded: "I guess you could say I'm a freelance agent; I go wherever He sends me. This King also has a book that's a world-wide bestseller."

"Did he write the book himself?" Jim asked. "Or did someone else write it for him?"

Bill explained that the book had been written by a number of authors. His new acquaintance got a gleam in his eye and said, "The King is Jesus, isn't it?"

"Yes," replied Bill.

"Tell me," he asked, "how did you get the job?"

Bill shared his story.

After he finished, the conversation ceased. Awhile later, the two men talked about lighter things. Near the end of the flight, remembering what the stranger had shared about himself, Bill asked two pointed questions.

First he said, "Jim, did your dad ever tell you that he loved you?"

Jim replied, no, he hadn't.

"Did your dad ever tell you that he was proud of you?"

Again Jim gave the same response.

Sensing the need to affirm this man, Bill said, "Jim, I know how committed you are to your wife and stepson; I know how hard you worked in school and how hard you labor at your job." Then Bill Smith did something remarkable. He reached out his hand and said, "Jim, I'm proud of you!"

The words struck a chord in this man's aching heart. He looked out the window—and brushed a tear from his eye.

The plane landed. The passengers departed. Jim lingered behind.

Finally rising from his seat, he reached into his briefcase and handed Bill his card. Then he said, "Bill, I'd like to know more about this King of yours. I may want to go to work for Him, too."

A Vision of Life That Connects
Time and Eternity

Do you know this King? Have you shared Him with your son? Only Jesus Christ satisfies the threefold criteria of a transcendent cause, as outlined in the Scriptures:

1. Jesus Christ is *truly heroic.* "And He was saying to them all, 'If anyone wishes to come after Me, he must deny himself, and take up his cross daily and follow Me. For whoever wishes to save his life will lose it, but whoever loses his life for My sake, he is the one who will save it' " (Luke 9:23-24).

2. Jesus Christ is *timeless.* "Jesus Christ is the same yesterday and today and forever" (Hebrews 13:8).

3. Jesus Christ is *supremely meaningful.* "Jesus said to him, 'I am the way, and the truth, and the life; no one comes to the Father but through Me' " (John 14:6). "Jesus again spoke to them, saying, 'I am the Light of the world' " (John 8:12).

Every son needs to hear his father say, "I love you." Every son needs to hear a father say—just as Bill Smith told Jim—that he's proud of him. These are good things. But every son needs more than that if he is to become a Modern-Day Knight.

Every son needs a transcendent cause, something that takes him beyond himself. Every son needs a vision for life that "integrates the end of life with the beginning," a vision for life that connects time and eternity. And then, over time, this "boy-become-man" will be able to step into the autumn of life with a satisfying sense of dignity, significance, and well-being.

The Bible records that Abraham finished his life just this way. When he passed away at the age of 175, he "breathed his last and died . . . an old man and *satisfied with life*" (Genesis 25:8, emphasis added).

You can finish this way, too, Dad. So can your son. But it will take someone truly heroic, timeless, and supremely meaningful to get you there: *Jesus Christ!*

Key Moves for Presenting a Transcendent Cause to a Son

- First and foremost, share your faith with your son. Tell him how you became a Christian. Relate often to him why your faith is important to you and how Jesus Christ is impacting your life now. Tell him your story!

- Go through *The Quest for Authentic Manhood* video curriculum with some other dads. For more information, go to www.mensfraternity.com. This will equip you to teach your son about manhood from a Christian perspective.

- Join with other dads and take your sons through a basic Bible study on living the Christian life. Today's youth need Christian basics.

- Pray with your son on a regular basis. Let him sense your heart before God.

- Participate in your son's baptism. (Chapter 10 explains more fully how this can be done.)

- Share what you're learning from the Bible.

- Let your son see you serve God. Let him see you use your gifts in some specific way that furthers the kingdom of God, such as helping the poor, working with your church, taking a courageous moral stand, sharing your faith with a neighbor or friend, or praying for others.

Part III

The Knight and His Ceremonies

CHAPTER 7

THE POWER OF CEREMONY

Every knight remembers [his dubbing] as the
finest [day] of his existence.

—GEORGES DUBY

During my 30-plus years in the ministry, I've preached hundreds of sermons and led more Bible studies, counseled more people, and attended more planning meetings than I care to count. While I have many warm memories from these experiences, they are not as clear in my mind as those special moments that occurred during *ceremonies*. Yes, ceremonies.

I remember the tears of a baptismal candidate as he shared his newfound faith in Christ. I recall the testimony of friends and family members at the funeral of a devout Christian. Of course, I also recall certain ceremonies that I wish I could forget, like the times when I forgot my lines, or said something stupid, or when something blatantly *un*ceremonial occurred.

At a wedding where I officiated a few years ago, shortly after the bride came down the aisle, I realized we were in big trouble. I looked at the groom, and he looked right *through* me. I wasn't five minutes into the ceremony when this husband-to-be, on the biggest day of his life, fell backward in a swoon and crashed to the floor!

As you can imagine, the bride was aghast. Tottering between concern and humiliation, she tried to bolster her courage. The congregation looked anxiously toward the platform. Meanwhile, the groom's father and his attendants (several of whom were doctors) leaped to work, feverishly attempting to revive their unconscious comrade. They slapped his face and yelled at him—all to no avail.

The makeshift paramedic unit determined that the groom needed to get blood to his brain. (I later learned that a friend had given him a tranquilizer to calm his nerves, but the drug unfortunately made his blood rush from his head, causing him to lose consciousness.) Incredibly—in the sight of the entire congregation—they lifted him by his feet. As they did, his pants rolled up, exposing his hairy legs. I'll never forget the sight of this poor fellow, dressed in a tuxedo, dangling upside down like a side of beef in front of hundreds of people. The scene was so bizarre that the congregation burst into laughter.

Ten minutes later, the groom returned to the land of the living. But only momentarily. The ceremony began again. And again he fainted.

This was simply too much for the bride. She sobbed uncontrollably. When the groom came around the second time, we propped him up in a chair. I dispensed with the formalities and cut to one simple statement: "Do you take this woman to be your lawfully wedded wife?"

The groom mumbled, "Uh-huh."

"Congratulations . . . I think!" I said as a benediction. The groom was then hoisted and carried out of the church, while the bride was comforted by her mother and friend. With that, the new couple began their exciting new life together. (I should mention that their marriage endured—as did a videotape that probably would win the $100,000 prize on *America's Funniest Home Videos.*)

SEALED BY A CEREMONY

Ceremonies are those special occasions that weave the fabric of human existence. Weddings. Award banquets. Graduations. The day you became an Eagle Scout or were accepted into a fraternity. *We remember because of ceremony.*

Think back upon the significant moments in your life. With few exceptions, the value of those moments was sealed by ceremonies. Someone took the time to plan the details, prepare the speech, and purchase the awards—so you would feel special.

Ceremony should be one of the crown jewels for helping a boy become a man. In many cultures throughout history, a teenage boy has been taken through some type of ritual to mark his official passage into manhood. I believe one of the great tragedies of Western culture today is the absence of this type of ceremony.

I cannot even begin to describe the impact on a son's soul when a key manhood moment in his life is forever enshrined and memorialized by a ceremony with other men. I have been privileged to observe it in my sons' lives and in the lives of many others. In fact, what I will share in the following chapters are our powerful experiences in using ceremony to shape a boy's life and direction. You will want to listen closely here, Dad. This is "user-friendly stuff" that could result in some of your greatest moments with your son.

DIG, SET, SPIKE!

In the previous section of the book, we identified the three ideals of modern-day knighthood: a vision for manhood, a code of conduct, and a transcendent cause. These "weapons of the spirit" are transmitted from father to son through *character, instruction,* and *ceremony.* Each component is critical.

A volleyball analogy will be helpful. As you know, when the ball is hit over the net, three shots are expected for a team to score a point. The first is called the "dig." Digging is grunt work. It usually involves getting on your knees and absorbing a spike from the other team.

I compare digging to the unpleasant, often painful, formation of a father's character. A good dig puts the ball in play and allows a team to go on the offensive. So it is with a father's godly character. The dad who is sincere, honest, loving, and faithful puts himself in a position to influence his son for Christ.

The second shot is called the "set." Setting is a strategic move, requiring precision and finesse, and it sets the stage for the spike. A father's everyday instruction is like this strategic set. Boys need to be instructed and trained in the ideals of knighthood. They need to be taught, from Dad's lips, what a man is, how a man should conduct himself, and what a man should live for. This part, too, requires precision and finesse.

After the dig and the set—*and only then*—are we ready for the "spike." The spike is an aggressive, powerful play. When a player rises to the net and spikes the ball into the other court, he puts an exclamation point on his team's execution. A good spike finalizes everything his team has worked so hard to accomplish.

A ceremony is like the spike. It drives home the point with unmistakable certainty.

Our medieval counterparts understood this all too well. While a knight's identity was shaped by instruction, his journey to manhood was "spiked" by an elaborate act of ceremony.

Historian Will Durant describes this memory-making event, known as a "dubbing":

> The candidate began with a bath as a symbol of spiritual, perhaps as a guarantee of physical, purification. . . . He was clothed in white tunic, red robe, and black coat, representing respectively the hoped-for purity of his morals, the blood he might shed for honor or God, and the death he must be prepared to meet unflinchingly.
>
> For a day he fasted; he passed a night at church in prayer, confessed his sins to a priest, attended Mass, received communion, heard a sermon on the moral, religious, social, and military duties of a knight, and solemnly promised to fulfill them.
>
> He then advanced to the altar with a sword hanging from his neck; the priest removed the sword, blessed it, and replaced it upon his neck. The candidate turned to the seated lord from whom he sought knighthood, and was met with a stern question: "For what purpose do you desire to enter the order? If it be riches, to take your ease, and be held in honor without doing honor to knighthood, you are unworthy of it."
>
> The candidate was prepared with a reassuring reply. Knights or ladies then clothed him in a knightly array of

hauberk, breastplate, armlets, gauntlets (armored gloves),
sword, and spurs. The lord, rising, gave the accolade—three
blows with the flat of the sword upon the neck or shoulder,
and sometimes a slap on the chest, as symbols of the last
affronts that he might accept without redress; and "dubbed"
him with the formula, "In the name of God, St. Michael, and
St. George I make thee knight."

The new knight received a lance, a helmet, and a horse; he
adjusted his helmet, leaped upon his horse, brandished his
lance, flourished his sword, rode out from the church, distrib-
uted gifts to his attendants, and gave a feast for his friends.[1]

Dig . . . set . . . spike. He was now a knight!

Do you think this young man would ever wonder if he *really*
became a knight?

Would you ever find him in a dark corner of some medieval
tavern, anxiously wrestling with the question, "Who am I?" I don't
think so.

To this powerful quotation let me add one more by Richard Barber. Read the words slowly; drink in every syllable. This is precisely
what our society's sons are missing.

From the early days of knights who were simple fighting men
to the extravaganza of the most elaborate kind of chivalry, the
ceremony of knighting was the central moment in a knight's
life. Its roots lay in the initiation ritual, by which primitive
societies marked the coming of age of adolescents.[2]

We need celebrations like this today to mark the passages from
adolescence to manhood. *Boys need manhood ceremonies that will live*

on in their memory—elaborate occasions that will "spike" forever the defining moments of the passage to modern-day knighthood. *Your son needs them, Dad!*

WHAT MAKES A GOOD CEREMONY?

Ceremonies come in all shapes and sizes. But the truth is, *good* ceremonies share four common characteristics.

First, *memorable ceremonies are costly.* The more time, thought, planning, effort, and money you give to a celebration, the more memorable it will be.

For example, you can celebrate your wedding anniversary by giving your wife a nice card with your signature. You might get by with such a meager offering—but I doubt it! Or you can include roses with the card. Better still is a card, roses, and *dinner* at a nice restaurant.

But as every woman knows—and every man has discovered, usually the hard way—the best approach is even costlier, such as a card, roses, dinner, and a *poem* you took hours to write. In the language of ceremony, this constitutes a four-bagger, a grand slam. Memorability grows in proportion to cost. The more you give, the greater the impact.

Second, *memorable ceremonies ascribe value.* By setting aside time, making the effort, spending money, and employing meaningful ceremony, we declare the high value of an individual. At the same time, ceremonies ascribe value to the beliefs and morals we hold important. Effective ceremony says, *You are important!* and *This moment is important!* It ascribes dignity and worth.

Third, *memorable ceremonies employ symbols.* Weddings are symbolized by a ring, Christmas by a star, graduation by a diploma. Each of these symbols calls to mind a host of pleasant memories.

The most memorable wedding anniversary Sherard and I ever celebrated involved a diamond necklace she wears around her neck. The
most memorable Valentine's Day we ever celebrated included a poem
I wrote and read before the whole church to honor her—a poem that
is now framed and hangs on our dining room wall.

Finally, and perhaps most importantly, *memorable ceremonies
empower a life with vision.* The wedding ceremony points to a new life
of one rather than two; the graduation ceremony envisions a new
career; the fraternity ceremony, a new circle of friends; father-child
ceremonies, a new stage of life. Ceremony marks the transition from
one season to another. It says powerfully, forcefully, and *regally,* "From
this point forward, life is going to be different!"

At the conclusion of Dostoevsky's classic *The Brothers Karamazov,*
Alyosha consoles a group of boys who are grieving over the death of a
friend. He says this about memories:

> I want you to understand, then, that there is nothing nobler,
> stronger, and healthier, and more helpful in life than a good
> remembrance, particularly a remembrance from our childhood,
> when we still lived in our parents' house. You often hear people
> speak about upbringing and education, but I feel that a beauti-
> ful, holy memory preserved from early childhood can be the
> most important single thing in our development. And if a per-
> son succeeds, in the course of his life, in collecting many such
> memories, he will be saved for the rest of his life. And even if
> we have only one such memory, it is possible that it will be
> enough to save us some day.[3]

I wonder: Do you treasure any ceremonial memories that marked
your passage from adolescence to manhood? That empowered it with

vision? Will many of the young boys growing up right now in our culture experience such a moment?

Most men in our society today lack a rich, masculine memory because there are no manhood ceremonies. Instead of *lasting* impressions, there are *no* impressions—no powerful, internal portraits etched in memory that call to mind our passage to manhood, no indelible moments that shaped our masculine identity and now compel us to pursue authentic manhood.

THE LEGACY OF MANHOOD

Let me tell you how a friend of mine created a special memory for his stepson.

Chris Lott was 19 when his mother married Dale Kinzler. At first, as in any blended family, Chris's relationship with Dale was awkward. But the two men had two things in common: a love for the Lord, and a love for Jimmilee—Chris's mom and Dale's wife.

While attending our Men's Fraternity group, Dale realized the importance of affirming his stepson as a man. Along with another father-son team, Dale and Chris planned a backpacking trip to the Ouachita Mountains in central Arkansas.

During the four-mile hike to their campsite, the fathers asked their sons to think up a list of all the things children do. They wanted them to visualize the immature behavior of youth.

Around the campfire that night, the boys were instructed to write down their lists, place them in an envelope, and throw them into the fire—which they did. This symbolized their break with childhood and their initiation into manhood.

The teenagers were then presented with gold "credit cards." Chris found his name printed in the center of the card under the words

"Affirmation of Membership in the Legacy of Manhood." The symbol of a compass was printed on the two upper corners of the card, but in one compass the familiar designations for north, south, east, and west were replaced by crosses. This signified new direction for their lives.

On the lower left-hand corner of Chris's card were the words "Dale Kinzler, Earthly Father." In the lower right-hand corner, the words "Jesus Christ, Heavenly Father." And summarizing this transition to manhood, the card included a reference to 1 Corinthians 13:11: "When I was a child, I used to speak as a child, think as a child, reason as a child; when I became a man, I did away with childish things."

Dale concluded the ceremony by explaining the importance of each of the symbols. Then the fathers prayed for their sons.

Later that year, on Father's Day, Dale received this letter from Chris:

> Dear Dad,
> I know I wasn't born your son, but by God's amazing grace, He has made two separate families one. And I thank Him every day for that. I want more than anything for you to know that I'm thankful for you. I'm thankful because you came along and loved my mom with all your heart and soul. You changed her life and mine.
> I know your legacy isn't over, but you have already started a legacy in me, whether you know it or not. In your life, you've taught me what it means to be a godly man, and I know I'm not finished learning.
> When I think of Dale Kinzler, I think of a man who deserves respect, a man of character, a man of integrity, a man

you can trust, a man of his word, and a man who always has a story to tell. In all, when I think of you, I think of a man who is committed to God.

I'll never forget our camping trip to the Ouachita Mountains when you really affirmed me as a son and as a man. Someday, when and if I have a son, we'll go on a camping trip just like that, and then you and I can induct him into our "Legacy of Manhood."

Proverbs 22:1 says, "A good name is more desired than great riches, favor is better than silver and gold." With much prayer and consideration, it is my wish to honor you by taking on your last name and carrying on your legacy in my life.

With much appreciation, your son,

Chris

Dale keeps copies of Chris's letter in his office at work and in his study at home. He also has a miniature version in his wallet. When asked what he thought of his son's letter, Dale said simply, "In my whole life, I have never received a better one."

Welcome, Dale Kinzler, to the Power of Ceremony.

CHAPTER 8

FOUR KEY MANHOOD CEREMONIES

> When his apprenticeship was finished
> [the candidate for knighthood] was received into the
> knightly order by a ritual of sacramental awe.
>
> —WILL AND ARIEL DURANT

D avid Wills faced a monumental task. Governor Andrew Curtin of Pennsylvania appointed him to oversee the burial of thousands of Union and Confederate soldiers at Gettysburg. In addition, the 32-year-old attorney was to plan a dedication ceremony for this pivotal Civil War battle.

The task was daunting. Following the July 1863 conflict, Gettysburg had taken on the appearance—and the stench—of an open-air mortuary. Thousands of human bodies lay scattered over the fields and hills, decaying in the heat. Others were buried but, as Wills reported to Governor Curtin, "In many instances arms and legs and sometimes heads protrude, and my attention had been directed to several places where the hogs were actually rooting out the bodies and devouring them."[1] Human scavengers picked at the exposed bodies for anything of value. Meanwhile, grieving relatives scoured the fields, searching for fathers and sons. Gettysburg had become a "carnival of carnage." Like a scene from Dante's *Inferno*, the grisly features of death were pervasive, revolting, visceral.

Something had to be done. David Wills did it. But at every turn, he was like a man stumbling in the dark. He started by forming an interstate commission to finance the project. Seventeen acres were purchased for a cemetery, and a company was retained to exhume, prepare, and bury the bodies. (Wills had hoped to have the burial completed before the November ceremony, but it wouldn't be finished until the following spring.)

Having resolved the pressing issues of burial and hygiene, the agent turned his attention toward the ceremony itself. Wills desired to memorialize the sacrifices of these brave men by staging an elaborate ceremony. According to the conventional wisdom of his day, this entailed securing a powerful orator who could lend dignity to the event, someone who would speak for two hours (as was the custom) and bring a lofty perspective to the proceedings. Without question, Edward Everett was the man.

An Ivy League scholar and former Secretary of State, Everett was considered the preeminent orator of his generation. He had dedicated the battlefields at Lexington and Concord as well as Bunker Hill. Almost as an afterthought, David Wills also extended an invitation— two months later—to President Lincoln, with the request that Lincoln deliver only "a few appropriate remarks."

On November 19, 1863, an estimated 20,000 people gathered for the ceremony. They had traveled by horse, train, and carriage from as far away as Minnesota to participate in the event. Under a blue sky, Lincoln and Everett, along with a host of other dignitaries, sat on a raised platform amid a sea of onlookers.

The ceremony began. First there was music. Then a prayer. And more music. Then it was time for the keynote address. Edward Everett's presentation was worthy of his reputation. For two hours, he held the crowd in thrall with his fiery language, his childlike animation, and his detailed description of the battle.

Following a hymn, Lincoln stepped to the podium. "Four score and seven years ago," he began . . . and before anyone knew it, he was finished. The crowd, which hadn't expected much, was still surprised by the brevity of his speech. Historian Garry Wills, in his much-acclaimed book *Lincoln at Gettysburg*, alludes to the story of a photographer who, expecting the president to be at the podium for a while, missed his shot while he slowly set up his camera.[2] In 272 words, the president said what he wanted to say and then sat down. The choir sang a dirge, the Reverend H. L. Baugher gave the benediction, and it was over.

The rest, as they say, is history.

EXPECTING THE UNEXPECTED

I share this story to illustrate two important points that will guide and encourage you as you plan manhood ceremonies for your son. First, keep in mind that *creating ceremonies is an experimental process.* Like David Wills, you will be working in something of a vacuum. However, you can succeed. Later in this chapter, I will detail the four ceremonies that two other fathers and I have created for our sons. These are now fairly polished and refined. But it wasn't this way at the beginning. When we started this experimental process—much like David Wills—we didn't know what we were doing. All we had was a lofty objective: to ceremonialize a vision for manhood. Our final product developed over time, after much trial and error.

Second, *ceremonies produce surprises.* David Wills had no idea that Lincoln's speech—not Everett's—would be the defining moment at Gettysburg. Lincoln's participation was ancillary, almost accidental. Yet when we think of Gettysburg, we recall the "Gettysburg Address." Few of us have ever heard of Edward Everett.

The point is, the outcome of ceremonies can be surprising. This was true at Gettysburg; it is equally true of the manhood ceremonies with which we are familiar. In case after case, the testimony of sons about their manhood ceremonies verifies this important point. They express a feeling of awe. They are overwhelmed that their father, and others, would take the time and invest the money to create such memorable experiences.

As dads, we have been overwhelmed, too. The power of ceremony to reaffirm a son's shaky identity, in some cases redirect his life, and empower his future was wholly unexpected. We have been amazed at the powerful results of our small investment.

A FAMILY CREST

As I mentioned in Chapter 1, years ago I began meeting with two good friends, Bill Wellons and Bill Parkinson, to research, discuss, and plan how to raise our sons into manhood. Then Ann Parkinson asked me a question I couldn't answer. She said: "Robert, how does a young man *know* when he has become a man?" As the mother of three teenage boys, Ann wanted to know.

The more I thought about the question, the more I realized Bill, Bill, and I needed to do something to initiate our sons into manhood. Something tangible. Something memorable. With seven sons between us, we wanted to create something that would empower our boys. So the three concerned fathers got together and took tentative steps toward designing manhood ceremonies.

At our first meeting, someone mentioned the idea of creating a family crest. Bill Parkinson then independently researched the subject of heraldry and brought back some examples.[3] Using these as a guide, we fashioned a crest that reflected our values. Then we took our idea to Nancy Carter, a graphic artist employed by our church. Nancy played with the concept and the colors and developed the finished product. We then had three copies matted and framed and placed in prominent locations in our homes.

I've reproduced a copy for you here. As you can see, our crest is in the common form of a shield. The Greek words across the top say "Fight the good fight," an allusion to Paul's admonition in 2 Timothy 4:7. The helmet symbolizes the fight of faith. The Greek phrase at the bottom of the crest means, "One Lord, one faith, one hope."

Three major sections make up the crest. The section on the left— with the sword in the shape of a cross—represents the *conventional* manhood described in Chapter 6, a manhood that must be surrendered to Jesus Christ. The section on the right with the crown and wreath symbolizes *authentic* manhood, as defined in detail in Chapter 4. (The crown with three jewels stands for the three imperatives of real manhood: rejecting passivity, accepting responsibility, leading courageously; the wreath below stands for the promise of greater reward, God's reward.) The three swords in the middle represent not only our three families, but the ongoing masculine truths each dad offers a son to fight with for an honorable life.

COMMEMORATING KEY PASSAGES IN A BOY'S LIFE

We now had a major *symbol*, but we still lacked a *process*. As our discussions continued, the three of us identified some key passages in a boy's journey to manhood. With our own experiences as a plumb line, we settled upon these four:

1. *Puberty*—that great transition at the start of adolescence when a boy's body wreaks havoc with his mind.

2. *High school graduation*—when, for the first time, a young man experiences unbridled freedom.

3. *College graduation*—when a man must face the world and begin to provide for himself. (If your son chooses not to attend college, identify a similar milestone: completion of a vocational training program; beginning of a career-oriented job; conclusion of a military assignment.)

4. *Marriage*—when a man assumes responsibility for a wife and the leadership of a family.

We then decide to craft ceremonies to commemorate these passages and to empower each of our sons with a vision for the next stage.

PUBERTY: THE PAGE STAGE

Age 13 is a pivotal time in a boy's life. A chemical called testosterone, the male sex hormone, which has always been present in smaller amounts, begins to appear in large quantities. Testosterone triggers the development of muscle tissue and transforms a boy's physical features. It breeds whiskers and pubic hair, and often promotes rapid growth.

But the changes are not just physical. As Dr. James Dobson writes in his book *Parenting Isn't for Cowards:*

> I believe parents and even behavioral scientists have underestimated the impact of the biochemical changes occurring in puberty. We can see the effect of these hormones on the physical body, but something equally dynamic is occurring in the brain. How else can we explain why a happy, contented, cooperative twelve-year-old suddenly becomes a sullen, angry, depressed, thirteen-year-old?[4]

At this stage in his development, a boy's body often outpaces his ability to comprehend the changes taking place inside him. Puberty is a confusing time for a young man. His sexual desires become intense and predominating. A boy needs a father's help to make sense of the confusion.

Before my oldest son, Garrett, turned 13, I asked him to join me in listening to and discussing Dr. Dobson's tape series called "Preparing for Adolescence." This seven-part study covers such issues as emotions, physical changes, sex, and self-esteem. We went to the church in the early mornings for our study, then concluded our times with breakfast at a local restaurant. Each session, including breakfast, took approximately two hours. It was a great time of preparing Garrett for this personally significant transition he was about to experience.

Our talks were lively, sometimes explicit (we talked candidly about sex), and relationally bonding for father and son. At the conclusion of our study (which I coordinated with his thirteenth birthday),

I prepared a simple ceremony and took Garrett to dinner and let him order any meal on the menu. He chose his favorite: steak.

For an hour, the two of us sat and talked about adolescence and manhood and his growing responsibilities. At this time, I introduced the manhood definition we covered in Chapter 4: "A man is someone who rejects passivity, accepts responsibility, leads courageously, and expects the greater reward—God's reward." I explained these phrases and illustrated each concept in a simple way.

I then asked Garrett to memorize the definition, which he did almost immediately. I told him this would be the "north star" for his manhood and that I planned to refer to it often in the years ahead. We then finished this special ceremonial occasion with my prayer for God's blessing in his life.

Reinforcing the Lesson

The unexpected surprises from that ceremony came later. Since that time, I've been amazed at how many opportunities I've had to shape my son's behavior by referring back to our definition of manhood. This is the beauty of clarifying and defining values.

I remember the time our family went to dinner and Garrett charged inside the restaurant, forgetting to hold the door for his mother and sisters. I stopped him in mid-stride and said, "Hey, what does a real man do in a situation like this?"

Garrett immediately said, "Well, Dad, I guess a real man *accepts responsibility* for the women he's with." Bingo!

"So, instead of charging into the restaurant," I replied, "act the gentleman and become the door holder."

Once you've defined manhood for your son, small day-to-day

experiences such as this become opportunities to reinforce a biblical portrait of manhood.

My wife, Sherard, told me a few months ago about a girl at school who took an interest in Garrett. Another young lady, acting as a mediator for this budding relationship, began calling him on the phone to explore the possibility of a romance with her friend.

Garrett pondered this for a while. Then one night he took charge and called the interested girl directly. He told her he couldn't be her boyfriend.

Sherard overheard the conversation (no, she wasn't listening on the other extension), and when Garrett hung up, she complimented him on the way he had handled the situation. Without hesitation— almost matter-of-factly—Garrett replied, "Mom, a real man must reject passivity and accept responsibility for things like this!"

Nothing warms a father's heart like *progress*.

Even our daughters, Elizabeth and Rebekah—both older than Garrett—have benefited from our ongoing discussion. They have heard us refer again and again to the characteristics of an authentic man. Whether they realize it or not, they are subconsciously forming an image of what real men are like.

HIGH SCHOOL GRADUATION: THE SQUIRE STAGE

A second ceremony occurs when a son finishes high school. This, too, is a pivotal time, fraught with potential dangers. Upon leaving home for college, a young man discovers a newfound sense of freedom. And unless he is well-grounded, he may choose to renounce the values of home. Biographer Jay Parini describes John Steinbeck's first year at Stanford University:

Steinbeck wanted desperately to break free from parental
bounds, and by midyear he was refusing to visit his parents
every weekend—much to their consternation. He cultivated a
sense of himself as a libertine; indeed, he seems to have made
a conscious point of straying from the narrow path his parents
laid down for him.[5]

Steinbeck's first year at college—and all of his subsequent years—
was filled with drink, free sex, and a host of contemptible behaviors,
a course considered more and more the norm for college-age males.
Because of this danger, our graduation ceremony gives our sons a
vision greater than personal pleasure; we want them to view their time
at college (or military service, work, etc.) as a great opportunity to
make a mark for Christ, not for self.

All of our sons (see Chapter 13) have now been through our high
school graduation ceremony. It has had a profound effect upon each
of their lives. The three dads took each of these young men to a nice
restaurant (as you've discovered, food is a critical component of our
ceremonial format!) and celebrated this major passage in their lives
over dinner. Then, in a formal way, we talked with each son about a
number of issues pertinent to leaving home and continuing his education at college—which they all have. Each father openly shared about
his own collegiate successes and failures; we described honestly and in
detail the things we did wrong, the things we did right, and how these
things impacted our lives later on. We also discussed what we would
choose to do over if we could, with our wisdom of experience.

It was immediately clear that having *a group of dads* share like this
dramatically increased the power of this moment. (More about that in
Chapter 11, when I address knighthood and the community of men.)
We emphasized the importance of beginning strong academically, set-

From left: Me, Bill Wellons, Bill Parkinson, and Bill Parkinson, Jr. with our family crests

ting goals and boundaries, and resisting the host of temptations that awaited. Each son was given the opportunity to ask any questions on any subject. The interaction was often spirited and frank.

Then the three of us brought out a picture of our families' crest and explained select portions of the imagery to him. For instance, we used the three swords to represent one essential manhood truth from each dad that we wanted him to take along to college.

One of the truths we always communicated to our sons at this juncture was that we will no longer treat them as boys. From now on, our relationship will be more like peers. They are on their way to becoming men now and can be expected to be treated as such.

The discussion usually lasted for two hours or more. Once this part of the evening ended, we returned to one of our homes, where all the other members of the three families had gathered. We then pulled everyone into a circle around the college-bound son. Each father talked generously about this young man's achievements and character,

Our three families gathered at the conclusion of one of our manhood ceremonies

affirming his commitment to Christ. Other family members were invited to make special comments, too. Then everyone laid hands on this young man and prayed for him. Awesome!

"I'LL NEVER FORGET IT!"

In describing the impact of this one evening, Bill Wellons, Jr., said things such as "It was incredibly affirming. . . . It made me feel important. . . . It was really challenging."

Ben Parkinson echoes Bill's statements. By his own admission, Ben has always been skeptical about ceremonies. Ben said that his dad, a big movie buff, "is the kind of guy who will watch the movie *Glory* and then initiate a three-hour discussion. When I first heard about this knighthood business, I thought to myself, *Did Dad see the movie* First Knight *and get inspired?*"

But Ben's skepticism faded quickly when he personally went through the ceremony described above. He discovered that now, for the first time, he was answerable for his decisions. Dad wouldn't be looking over his shoulder anymore.

Another powerful effect has been the way Bill, Jr., and Ben view the other two dads. Said Bill, Jr., "After that night, every time I returned home from school, I couldn't wait to tell Mr. Parkinson and Mr. Lewis what I was learning. And every time I saw them, they were quick to ask how things were going."

Said Ben, "The other two dads became mentors for me. I knew if I had a problem, I could go to them and talk about it."

Both Bill, Jr., and Ben were awed by the process. That their fathers would take the time to plan the ceremony and share their hearts with them has left a profound mark.

College Graduation: The Knight Stage

This third ceremony is unique for three important reasons. First, it is here that we formally initiate our sons into manhood. Youth ends here. The ceremony takes an evening—or even a full weekend—of private interaction, when we discuss in depth this new life of independence and the responsibilities that come with it. We spend time defining additional aspects of the family crest, especially the crown and wreath, which depict authentic manhood. More than ever before, we challenge him to aspire to it, for *now is the time.* Reject passivity! Accept responsibility! Lead courageously! And again, the son is given the opportunity to ask questions, with robust interaction often taking place.

This ceremony is also unique because of a special gift. At the appropriate time, the young man's father reaches into his pocket and presents his son with a powerful reminder of this moment. A ring. But not just any ring. A ring of great value.

Applying the first rule of ceremonies ("Memorable ceremonies are costly"), we took our family crest to a jeweler and asked him to engrave this image on a gold ring. It cost nearly $1,000, and the three fathers contributed equally toward the expense. Like nothing else we do, this costly gift "spikes" forever in a young man's mind the importance of the occasion. It is his dubbing as a knight.

The ring we use to mark
manhood in our sons

The college graduation ceremony was the first milestone marker for Bill Parkinson, Jr., (we developed the process after he had graduated from high school). He was absolutely floored by the experience. He told his dad afterward that the whole evening was a blur and said he didn't remember half of the things that Bill, Bill, and I had said to him. He asked if we could write down the things we had shared, which we did.

During the family meeting at home that night, Bill, Jr., kept looking at his ring, pulling it off his finger, and admiring the design. Later, he confided that this ceremony was a major turning point in his life.

For Ben Parkinson, this ceremony was just as profound. He said the ring "became a symbol of manhood and of my commitment to Christ." As Ben reflected upon that evening, he realized that the reason he was secure in his faith, his values, and in himself was because his parents were committed to these same ideals.

JOINING THE ROUND TABLE

The college graduation ceremony is special for one more reason. Once a son has been through this ceremony, he formally joins the dads as a "fellow knight." He is now to be included in their round table. For the first time, he becomes an active participant in the other manhood ceremonies with the younger sons as they reach these same milestones.

Once Bill Parkinson, Jr., had completed his ceremony, he was able to be present when his brother Ben went through his manhood initiation. It meant a lot to Ben to see Bill there and to hear him share his growing manhood experiences. Before long our round table grew from three knights to six.

This particular ceremony continued to evolve. Our goal was to make the college graduation ceremony a weekend event instead of an evening. We wanted to get away for at least two days and discuss key manhood concepts that I regularly present in my Men's Fraternity materials. That, plus some manly activities (hunting, fishing) and leisurely discussions would make our initiation into manhood even more memorable.

MARRIAGE: THE PROMISE/OATH STAGE

I have already described this ceremony at some length in the conclusion of Chapter 1. It may be helpful to you at this point to go back and reread what we did as one son entered the bonds of matrimony. This was the only ceremony that went "public," that is, occurred before someone other than the immediate families.

Remember, one of the primary responsibilities of real manhood revolves around "a woman to love." You may also remember that a knight's promise—his word of honor—was the most important thing a knight possessed. Knights were the Promise Keepers of the Middle Ages.

A woman to love and one's *word of honor.* Both elements are central to this final ceremony that occurs the night before the wedding, at the rehearsal dinner.

In one promise/oath ceremony we conducted, Ben Parkinson was challenged in the ways of married manhood by each of the dads. Then, to "spike" this special moment, he and his bride-to-be received a family crest like the one in each of our homes, for the new home they were creating together as husband and wife.

Two final exhortations concluded this ceremony. First, Ben was exhorted as a knight to keep the vows he would make to Aimee the following day. Second, he was exhorted to keep the vow he had already made to us: the promise of pursuing manhood for a lifetime.

This is what *we* do. There is nothing sacrosanct about our ceremonies; you may choose to imitate aspects of these or develop your own. But the important thing is that you *do something* creative and memorable to initiate your son into manhood. Remember, too, that the power of the ceremony is the *actual experience!* It is the lingering memory it makes and in the potent vision it marks.

IF ONLY SOMEONE WOULD NOTICE . . .

General Ulysses S. Grant, whose victories at Vicksburg, Chattanooga, and elsewhere sealed the conflict for the Union, is considered one of the heroes of the War between the States. But Grant's success is remarkable when you consider his background.

You see, prior to the war, Ulysses S. Grant was a confirmed failure. He had failed as a farmer, a peddler of firewood, and as the proprietor of a leather store in Galena, Illinois. At one point, he was so broke that he pawned his gold watch—a family heirloom—for $22.

But deep in his heart, Ulysses S. Grant *knew* he could succeed. William S. McFeely, in his Pulitzer Prize–winning biography, makes this powerful observation: "[Grant] had, all along, ideas and a [good] sense of himself that *he could make no one notice*" [emphasis added].[6] No matter how hard Grant tried, no one seemed to sense his potential.

Many sons today are just like Ulysses S. Grant. They have a sense of themselves, a premonition that they were created for something significant, *if only someone would notice them!*

Someone like a father. With great clarity and regal pronouncement, manhood ceremonies tell a son, "I notice you! You are important to me! You are important to the kingdom of God! You have an important masculine destiny to fulfill!"

You can do it, Dad! Take the time to craft some ceremonies for your son. Make them costly. Make them memorable. Celebrate!

He'll remember these special occasions *with you* as some of the finest days of his life.

CHAPTER 9

OTHER MANHOOD CEREMONIES TO CONSIDER

Society expected each man to aspire constantly to
chivalric behavior; in return, they gave him an
honorable place in the union of men.

—ARNO BORST, *MEDIEVAL WORLDS*

C eremonies make powerful memories. I saw this several years
ago when I set about creating a special ceremony to honor my
parents.

After reading my personal story back in Chapter 2, you may wonder why I would ever do such a thing, when my childhood was filled
with such turmoil. What motivated me was a sermon by my friend

Dennis Rainey on the fifth commandment: "Honor your father and mother."

As I listened to Dennis speak, I realized God hadn't called His people to honor only "good" parents with unblemished records. We were to honor them regardless of their failures and inconsistencies. Dennis also mentioned that many adults, like myself, who grew up in severely dysfunctional homes seem to remember only the bad times; they forget the things their parents did right.

Those words hit home, and over the next few months I began to look at my parents through a different lens. It was a long and painful process; I didn't gloss over the pain they had caused, but I also began to remember the good as well. I began to feel compassion for them as I tried to understand their situation.

I ended up writing a tribute entitled "Here's to My Imperfect Family" in which I acknowledged the struggles our family went through, but I also thanked them for their work, their sacrifices, the good memories they did create for us, and for staying together through terrible hardships. For me, writing that tribute was both an emotional and a freeing experience. But I also knew I needed to present it to my parents in a way that would be freeing for them.

That chance came on Christmas Day. Sherard, the kids, and I had made the traditional drive to Ruston to see our parents who lived there. After we opened our gifts with Mom and Dad, I pulled out the tribute—matted and framed—and said to them, "There are a lot of things I've always wanted to say to you that I've never known how to say. So I've tried my best to put them all into writing. I'd like to read it to you."

And that's what I did, with my wife and children at my side.

I had to stop several times because my eyes filled with tears. I looked over at Dad, and I saw his eyes welling up, too. He didn't quite cry, but he was obviously touched. Mom just sat there, stunned, with tears rolling down her face. She couldn't believe—after all we had been through—that I was actually honoring her for the good things she had done as a mother.

When I finished, we all just sat there, not knowing what to say. Nothing like this had ever happened in the Lewis family. But we all knew it was a *holy* moment of honor and healing. The next day, when I returned to their house, the first thing I saw was my framed tribute hanging in the most prominent spot in the home.

Little did I know that just nine months later my father would die of a heart attack. Therefore, I will always thank God for this moment we had together.

Ceremonies are powerful moments that mark our lives. To be effective, they need a handcrafted, personalized touch. In the previous two chapters, I've described for you some of the manhood ceremonies Bill, Bill, and I have used with our sons. In this chapter, I'd like to broaden your perspective.

Manhood ceremonies can come in all shapes and sizes, varying from family to family. Here are five additional ones used by men in our church. Each is different, but all are powerful and memorable.

A NIGHT TO REMEMBER

When Clay Freeman turned 18, he experienced one of the greatest days of his life. His father, Steve, informed his son a few days before that they were going to do something special. Steve had been thinking about and planning this event for a few years.

Steve invited four key Christian men to participate: Clay's uncle, his small-group leader, his pastor, and the missions pastor who had accompanied Clay on two short-term trips. One November evening the group gathered at the Freeman home for dinner. Then the ceremony began.

One by one, the four adult friends talked with Clay about different components of manhood. The missions pastor discussed the significance of turning 18 and the responsibilities that accompanied this new stage. He identified many positive qualities in Clay: his uprightness, his faithfulness, his perseverance, and his high regard for others.

The uncle talked about the importance of attitude and shared a powerful quotation by Chuck Swindoll. He challenged Clay to work on being positive and not to get down on himself.

The small-group leader identified seven characteristics of a real man and illustrated his points from the book of Joshua.

Finally, the pastor discussed the responsibilities of manhood, specifically the biblical admonition to *lead.*

When the other men finished, Steve finally spoke. Taking out a sheet of paper, he read a blessing he had composed for his son. It concluded with this sentence: "I seal this blessing tonight with a handshake and an embrace. Not the embrace of a father and a boy, but man-to-man. I am proud of you, my son."

Following the blessing, which made both father and son cry, the group gathered around Clay and prayed for him. The male mentors then signed a certificate of initiation into manhood and presented it to Clay. Finally, they concluded the evening by taking pictures.

Clay, normally a soft-spoken teenager, was exuberant about the evening. And in its aftermath, he made some critical decisions. First, he committed himself to become a better student of the Scriptures. Second, he determined to "act like a man"—to become more responsible for himself and for others. Finally, Clay took to heart the charge by his uncle to honor God with his attitudes. For this young man, it was a life-changing experience.

SURPRISES IN THE WOODS

When Allan Mesko drove his son, Brian, to the Ozark Conference Center about an hour west of Little Rock, the 16-year-old thought he and his dad were simply going to "spend the night on the mountain." But Allan had other plans.

They checked in with the couple who managed the camp, and soon this couple's son invited Brian to go for a walk. As the two teenagers strolled down a path, suddenly the headmaster at Brian's Christian school stepped out from behind a tree. Brian's first thought was, *He must be staying at the lodge.*

But after a quick greeting, the other boy returned home. Brian and his headmaster continued walking, the older man explaining that Brian's father had asked him to share some thoughts on the subject of manhood. Bible in hand, he turned to the books of 1 and 2 Timothy and highlighted specific passages relevant to manhood.

After a while, the two came to a teepee. Brian saw a pair of feet inside the tent. Soon a new escort took the headmaster's place. Walking past ponds and through open meadows, this man talked with Brian about the different choices he would face as a man. He also made a statement Brian will never forget. He said, "Brian, maybe one day you'll be doing this walk with my son."

The pair headed into the woods, where an older teacher at Brian's school was seated on a bench. His part was to cover the characteristics of manhood. After a while, the two headed back to the lodge, with Brian assuming that the surprises were now over.

They weren't. Four other adult friends were at the lodge waiting for him. Allan grilled some expensive steaks, and the celebrants drank soft drinks out of Mason jars. After dinner, the group gathered in a circle, and each man shared special qualities they had noticed in Brian.

The young man was speechless. Several times throughout the evening, he muttered, "I don't know what to say."

Allan then presented his son with James Dobson's book *Life on the Edge*, signed by all the men. He also gave his son a plaque, which read:

To my son, Brian Benjamin Mesko, in recognition of your initiation into the community of men, July 11, 1995, Ozark Conference Center, with much love and great joy—Dad

The plaque also bears the inscription of 2 Timothy 2:1: "You therefore, my son, be strong in the grace that is in Christ Jesus." To conclude the ceremony, the men gathered around Brian and prayed for him.

Before they left the camp the next morning, Allan and Brian walked the same course Brian had traveled the evening before. The young man repeated what he'd heard and pointed out the key locations. Later, while Brian was occupied with the camp manager's son, Allan drove the same course in his car *again* to take pictures. He later presented the photographs to Brian.

"The evening exceeded my expectations!" Allan Mesko said upon reflection.

His son added, "When I think about that night, I am overwhelmed with joy. I'm so grateful for a dad who would do something like that."

A Powerful Gift

When Jerry Richardson's son, Cliff, turned 16, Jerry planned a ceremony that capitalized on their common passion for hunting. This father-and-son team has hunted together ever since Cliff was old enough to handle a gun.

One evening, on a farm Jerry owns, he and Cliff gathered for dinner with three longtime hunting partners. Afterward, each man talked to Cliff about manhood, sharing experiences from the past and biblical truths. Jerry had written out a list of manhood values he wanted Cliff to embrace—such things as honesty, sacrificial giving, respecting women, and giving to the community. Jerry framed these values and inscribed them on a plaque, which he presented to his son.

To "spike" the evening, Jerry gave Cliff something he'd wanted for a long time—a brand-new Ruger over-and-under shotgun. Cliff's eyes grew huge when he opened the gift. Jerry commented that a shotgun is a little like manhood: a powerful weapon that can be used for great good. But he also pointed out the dark side. A shotgun, when used improperly, can cause great destruction—and so it is with a man who lives only for himself.

In one memorable moment, this treasured possession became much more than a gun. It was transformed into a symbol of manhood.

Both of Cliff's grandfathers were also present at the ceremony, and they contributed meaningfully to the discussion. The group concluded their time together by laying hands on Cliff and praying for him.

LIGHTS ON THE RIVER

The Ford Explorer meandered slowly down the gravel road and halted at a wooden bridge on the Ouachita River near Friendship, Arkansas. On this cold November night, Bob Snider suddenly turned toward his 16-year-old son and asked, "John Snider, do you want to become a man?"

The question was certainly odd. John replied with a tentative "Uh-huh."

Bob continued: "Well, then, I want you to get out and walk the rest of the way to the cabin."

The young man looked at his father as if he were crazy. It was another four miles to his uncle's cabin on the river! He also knew that wild animals inhabited these dark, cold woods.

Before the teenager could lodge a formal protest, his father added: "John, trust me on this one." Confused and thoroughly surprised, John stepped from the vehicle and walked across the bridge. His father turned the Explorer around and drove away in the dark.

When John got to the other side of the Ouachita River, his cousin suddenly stepped from the shadows. Flashlight in hand, Steve said, "John Snider, do you want to become a man?"

John doesn't remember his response, other than to be sure he didn't say no. The cousin invited John to walk with him down the road. He explained why he was there and began to talk about manhood. Specifically, he discussed the subject of fear and shared some of his own fears.

After a mile, John's youth pastor stepped out and asked the same question: "John Snider, do you want to become a man?"

Now he joined the pair, talking about perseverance. After another mile, another relative showed up to coach John on successful relationships. At the three-mile marker, John's uncle joined them and talked about maturity.

While all this was happening, John's father was driving 20 miles around the back way to begin preparing the cabin for John's formal initiation ceremony. First, he dragged a canoe 200 yards into the middle of a soybean field and positioned a flashlight shining straight up into the air. He also left instructions for John to follow.

He then got into a flat-bottom boat and rowed across the river. On the other side, Bob placed a brand-new Bible on a sandbar and again left instructions plus another flashlight pointing toward the night sky. Finally, Bob returned to the cabin to grill steaks.

Bob watched intently as John and his companions neared the cabin. A hundred yards away, John's grandfather approached him and, like the other four, asked if he wanted to become a man.

"In order to become a man," said he, "you must learn to love."

He then talked with John about relationships and described how he had fallen in love with John's grandmother.

The grandfather had recently suffered a stroke and so had to proceed at a slower pace. Bob says he will never forget, as long as he lives, the sight of his father holding his son's hand and leading the group into camp.

Once at the cabin, the initiation ceremony began. The men placed a backpack full of bricks on John's back and blindfolded him. He was then instructed to find his father. While the other men distracted John by yelling, "John, I'm over here, I'm over here," Bob whistled softly. This act symbolized learning to listen for the important things in life.

Next, John was told to "follow the light and obey the Word." He found the canoe in the middle of the field, read the instructions, and dragged it back to the river. With his father watching from the riverbank, John crossed the river, found the Bible, and memorized Psalm 24:3-5.

When he returned, Bob asked him this question: "John, who may ascend into the hill of the Lord and who may stand in His holy place?" John responded by quoting the rest of the passage.

Bob then told John that he had successfully completed the initiation rite. From this point on he would be treated like a man, not a boy. Back in camp, John enjoyed a steak dinner with this community of men and spent the rest of the evening listening to personal stories about their own journeys to manhood. The men also signed John's Bible.

The evening had a profound impact upon John. "That night, I got a big dose of what it means to be a man," he says. "I admire each of these men, and I want to be just like them. And every time I read my Bible, I remember the occasion."

Two years later, John Snider was one of two seniors at Pulaski Academy to win an award for "Excellence in Character." John has clearly taken to heart the lessons learned that evening and is actively seeking to follow the Lord Jesus Christ.

"WELCOME TO MANHOOD"

Ragan Sutterfield's sixteenth birthday was still months away, but already his father, Ken, was making plans to celebrate his son's transition to manhood.

Ken contacted 16 men whom Ragan respected—his grandfathers, a pastor, a schoolteacher, a scout leader, and others—and asked each one to write a letter to him. Ken wanted Ragan to benefit from the manhood wisdom of others. After these "heroes" mailed their letters to Ken, he collected them and placed them in an album entitled "Welcome to Manhood."

But Ken had other things in store for Ragan. For 16 consecutive days leading up to Ragan's birthday, Ken presented his son with a gift that represented some aspect of manhood. Each evening during dinner, the father gave his son a present and explained the symbolic significance of each gift.

The first evening, Ken gave Ragan a study Bible and explained that it was a "guide for life." The second night, he presented him with a compass and encouraged him to "always look to God for direction." Other gifts included leather work gloves ("always work hard and be dedicated"), a pocketknife ("always be prepared"), a flashlight ("remember the One who is the real Light"), and a journal (for recording his thoughts and reflections).

Then on Ragan's birthday, the family took him to a restaurant (appropriately named "Heroes"), and Ragan ordered his favorite meal. Afterward, Ken presented Ragan with the "Welcome to Manhood" album.

The entire experience had a profound effect on Ragan. He stayed up late the night of his birthday reading the 16 letters in the album. Ken and his wife, Jan, have spied Ragan reading and rereading it on numerous occasions.

Ragan keeps referring back to this landmark experience, and why not? It commemorated the night he was called into authentic manhood.

YOUR TURN

While each of the ceremonies detailed above is different, they do share common characteristics. You'll want to incorporate some into your own manhood ceremonies.

First, remember to *employ the element of surprise.* Like most of us, a young man loves surprises; they heighten the effect.

Second, *make the ceremony intensely spiritual.* Relate the truths that are communicated—from father to son and from mentor to protégé—directly to the Bible.

Third, *incorporate symbols to mark the moment.* Whether it be a ring or a Bible, a shotgun or a plaque, the symbol becomes an ever-present reminder of this timeless event.

Fourth, *include a blessing from Dad.* Verbalize it during the ceremony, and present it afterward in written form.

Finally, *involve other men.* I'll have more to say about that in Chapter 11.

As you consider preparing a manhood ceremony for your son, think through the following questions:

1. What upcoming moments in your son's life could be turned into special ceremonies (turning 13, 16, 18, graduating from high school or college, leaving home, baptism, a special getaway, special events, etc.)?

2. What elements from the ceremonies you have read about in this book could you use in a ceremony of your own?

3. What creative ideas do you have for a manhood ceremony with your son?

4. If you were to create one manhood ceremony for calling your son into manhood, what would it look like?

5. What symbol would he take with him from that ceremony to remind him of his manhood calling?

The manhood ceremonies in these two chapters are described for *your* encouragement. They offer wonderful examples of what a dad can do, wielding the sword of ceremony. With it, you can deposit vision, calling, and affirmation deep into a son's heart. So how about it, Dad? Take this challenge and create a ceremony for your son. It will be an unforgettable experience for him—and you.

CHAPTER 10

COMMEMORATING A TRANSCENDENT CAUSE

After being baptized, Jesus came up
immediately from the water . . . and behold,
a voice out of the heavens said,
"This is My beloved Son, in whom
I am well-pleased."

—MATTHEW 3:16-17

I f you could ask Jesus Christ *one* question, what would it be? Let me set the scene for you. Imagine yourself seated at His feet; you have His undivided attention. You can pose anything on your mind . . . a puzzling theological concept, perhaps, or a painful personal issue such as the death of a loved one . . . or maybe you'd like to know how the worlds were created, or why the righteous suffer. It's your choice.

But you get only *one* question, so choose wisely.

A fanciful scenario, I know. But even so, I know what *I'd* ask Jesus. I would say, "What would you consider to be *the finest moment of Your time on earth?*"

Not the most miraculous moment, nor even the most triumphant, but the *finest.*

Having raised the question, may I be so bold as to guess His answer?

I fully believe He would point to His *baptism.* Not His role in Creation. Not the feeding of the 5,000 or the resurrection of Lazarus. Not even His *own* resurrection.

His baptism.

WHY CHRIST'S BAPTISM WAS SO IMPORTANT

Listen to Matthew's account of this important event in Matthew 3:13–17, and pay special attention to the last verse:

> Then Jesus arrived from Galilee at the Jordan coming to John, to be baptized by him. But John tried to prevent Him, saying, "I have need to be baptized by You, and do You come to me?" But Jesus answering said to him, "Permit it at this time; for in this way it is fitting for us to fulfill all righteousness." Then he permitted Him.
>
> And after being baptized, Jesus came up immediately from the water; and behold, the heavens were opened, and he saw the Spirit of God descending as a dove and lighting on Him, and behold, a voice out of the heavens said, "This is My beloved Son, in whom I am well-pleased."

To understand the preeminence of this event in Jesus' life, we need to grasp three significant truths.

First, *Jesus Christ was (and is) the God-MAN.* I capitalize the word "man" because it is the aspect of Christ's nature most evangelicals overlook. C. Samuel Storms writes, "Evangelicals are quick to defend the truth that in Jesus Christ 'all the fullness of Deity lives in bodily form' (Col. 2:9), and rightly we should. But there is a tendency among us, in the interests of Christ's deity to minimize His humanity."[1]

In the mystical union of His being, Jesus Christ was fully God *and* fully man. The physical and emotional characteristics of human flesh were present in Jesus Christ. Scripture tells us that Jesus possessed a body (John 2:21). For this reason, He got hungry (Matthew 4:2) and thirsty (John 19:28) and grew weary (John 4:6). Jesus wept at the sadness of others (John 11:35) and prayed with loud crying (Hebrews 5:7). He was tempted as we are tempted, but without sin (Hebrews 2:18).

Jesus the *man* was needy. If this statement disturbs you, then you have overlooked Christ's humanity. As a man, Jesus Christ needed to be affirmed and encouraged. Seen in this light, the Father's word become profoundly significant.

Second, we must understand that *Jesus was the SON of God.* He was a *son.* Every son—Christ included—stands in a unique relationship to his father. As we discovered in Chapter 3, "The glory of sons is their fathers." If your father's praise matters to you, why should it have been any different for Jesus Christ?

"Oh, but He was God," you say. Yes, He was God. But He was also a man. And as with every man, His Father's opinion mattered. Greatly. At one of the most critical moments in His life, Jesus needed to hear a word of affirmation from His Father, a hearty word of praise that would buttress His confidence and bolster His courage.

Third, we must understand that *our Lord's MISSION began with*

His baptism. The act of baptism inaugurated the *purpose* for which He had entered the world. At His baptism, Jesus embraced His *transcendent cause.*

In his book *The Life and Times of Jesus the Messiah*, Alfred Edersheim writes:

> His previous life had been that of the Perfect Ideal Israelite—believing, unquestioning, submissive—in preparation for that which, in His thirteenth year, He had learned as its business. The Baptism of Christ was the last act of His private life; and, emerging from its waters in prayer, He learned: when His business was to commence, and *how* it would be done.[2]

Why do I see this as *the* preeminent event in Jesus' life? Because at His baptism, the two most important elements in a son's life—the embrace of a transcendent cause and a father's affirmation—came together in one unforgettable, breathtaking moment.

At His baptism, Jesus Christ embraced His *mission* and then heard His Father say, "I'm proud of you, My Son!" The *transcendent cause* was blessed, affirmed, and "spiked" by the Father's vocal affirmation. If He held any doubts about His course in life, they were vanquished in that one instance. Every temptation He would encounter and all of the hardships He would endure were immediately put into perspective. He embraced His mission, and He was affirmed by His Father, investing the moment with reverential awe.

I believe that one of the finest moments in any son's life is when he embraces his transcendent cause and then hears his father say, "I'm proud of you, my son! . . . I'm pleased with the course you've chosen in life! . . . You've chosen well!" What can be better than this?

A Ceremony to Commemorate
a Transcendent Cause

In Chapter 6, we unearthed the three components of a transcendent cause: (1) It is *truly heroic*, a noble endeavor, calling forth bravery and sacrifice; (2) it is *timeless*, containing significance beyond the moment; and (3) it is *supremely meaningful.*

We also discovered in Chapter 6 that only Jesus Christ meets the threefold criteria of a transcendent cause. He is the ultimate reality.

Consequently, the son who chooses to follow Christ deserves praise. He has made the most important decision of his life and, for this reason, deserves to be honored for it.

But how can a father commemorate a transcendent cause? How can he spike this life-changing commitment with reverential awe? By doing exactly what God the Father did with His Son: *Participating in his baptism and blessing his decision.*

Most Christians are familiar with the theological components of baptism. They may not always remember, however, that it declares the pursuit of a new life. Summing up his instruction on baptism in Romans 6, the apostle Paul concludes with this marvelous exhortation: "Therefore do not let sin reign in your mortal body so that you obey its lusts, and do not go on presenting the members of your body to sin as instruments of unrighteousness; but present yourselves to God as those alive from the dead, and your members as instruments of righteousness to God" (verses 12-13).

In these verses, Paul alludes to a component of baptism that is often overlooked. He says that from this moment forward, we are to "walk in newness of life" (Romans 6:4). Baptism represents our death to the self-ruled life and our submission to the rule of God, our willing embrace of His mission for us.

For the father who desires to raise a Modern-Day Knight, baptism presents a great opportunity to identify with, and affirm, a son on this most solemn occasion!

MORE THAN A CASUAL OBSERVER

I fully recognize that baptismal practices vary from church to church, and they are often based on deeply held convictions. I have no desire to cause conflict or disruption. Let me see if I can say this as generically as possible: *Find a way to be more than just a casual observer sitting in the tenth row at your son's baptism.*

If your church believes in baptizing children as infants, you will of course be standing there for the occasion. If your church believes, as mine does, in baptizing only after a conscious confession of faith in Christ, there are a number of things you can do. You might ask to say an introductory word and affirm your son's decision. You might ask to be present *in the water* with him. If you attended my church, you could even go through a baptism class with your son and baptize him yourself. Many of our fathers have done this.

I fondly recall one dad who stepped into the baptistery one Sunday morning with his three sons. This dad had come to Christ in midlife, after years of reckless, godless living. Yet there he stood—a new man, changed by Jesus Christ. The three sons he was about to baptize had not only observed his radical lifestyle changes, but also were now willing to embrace the Life-Giver and His life themselves.

Just the sight of this new knight and his sons standing there brought tears to our congregation. A whole family was being rewired spiritually. New knights were being launched to pursue the high calling of Christ.

If you have the opportunity to speak, I suggest that you recount for the congregation the positive character traits you see in your son that God can and will use. Relate the act of baptism to the new call of manhood he will be pursuing in Christ: a call to reject passivity, accept responsibility, lead courageously, and expect the greater reward—God's reward. You may want to explain the responsibilities that go along with his commitment to Christ.

And after you've shared your heart and your son has been baptized, you can conclude this holy ceremony with the same words God the Father spoke to His Son: "This is My beloved son, in whom I am well-pleased."

You might want to go even further and host a baptism celebration for your son after this ceremony—a reception or a special dinner of some kind.

If your words are sincere and arise from a heart filled with integrity, your son may well remember it as the finest day of his life!

No Greater Joy

My good friend Dennis Rainey, national director of FamilyLife Ministries, entered the baptistery with his 19-year-old son, Benjamin. Dennis began by quoting 3 John 4: "I have no greater joy than this, to hear of my children walking in the truth." He went on to say that Benjamin was indeed a young man committed to walking in the truth.

Benjamin then shared his testimony, explaining to the congregation that he'd become a Christian at an early age but had lived primarily for himself a good portion of his life. In the tenth grade, however, Benjamin made a critical decision. He realized that joy in life was found in pleasing God. So in a repentant state of mind, he took on a new spiritual aggressiveness, looking for opportunities to live for

Christ, obey Christ, and serve Christ. And for him, a new lifestyle was born.

Benjamin concluded his testimony by saying, "The greatest thing I can do with my life now is to love the Lord God with all my heart, soul, mind, and strength."

Then it was Dennis's turn. Fighting back tears, Dennis paraphrased Matthew 3:17 with a quivering lip. With his arm around his son, Dennis said, "Benjamin, your mother and I are *very pleased* with you!"

A father. A son. United in a transcendent cause in the waters of baptism.

Few things are better than this.

Part IV

The Knight and His Round Table

Chapter 11

Knighthood and the Community of Men

We few, we happy few, we band of brothers.
—William Shakespeare, *Henry V*

I magine a continuum with two ends. At the right is the word *Ideal* with the number *100* underneath it. This is the place where you'd like your son to arrive one day—with a clear and powerful vision for manhood, a masculine code of conduct, and a vibrant transcendent cause . . . not as abstract concepts, but as palpitating, personal convictions.

On the left is the word *Reality* and the number *0*. This is where your son is right now. He lacks these three qualities, being either young or uninformed.

As a concerned father, how are you going to move your son from the *real* to the *ideal?* From *0* to *100?*

If you are serious about your assignment, I suspect you'll make an effort, first of all, to clean out your own closet. You will take to heart the importance of your own character and lifestyle. The father who diligently improves his own character and spiritual life can jump-start his own son to, say, the 25-point mark on the continuum—it is *that* significant.

You can move your son even further along by instructing him in the three ideals of Modern-Day Knighthood (presented in Chapters 4-6): defining an Authentic Manhood Vision, clarifying a Code of Conduct, and nurturing his relationship with Jesus Christ to give him a Transcendent Cause. Each of these is worth, say, 10 points apiece.

Fathers and sons on one of our many duck hunts

Then, you will go on to craft some special ceremonies for your son, like those we illustrated in Chapters 7-10. As a whole, these contribute another 20 points to your son's maturation.

Having done all this—you're still only three-fourths of the way along the continuum. What's missing?

Answer: *The Community of Men.*

THE DANGER OF INDIVIDUALISM

The truth is, a father can do everything right and still miss the *ideal* because he's neglected to involve this most critical of elements.

We are much different from our forebears. Peter Laslett writes:

> Time was, and it was all time up to 200 years ago, when the whole of life went forward in the family, in a circle of loved, familiar faces, known and fondled objects, all to human size. That time has gone forever. It makes us very different from our ancestors.[1]

We have become a nation of individuals. The community—which in ages past defined manhood, nurtured its development, and deepened its roots—is now a silent, forgotten bystander.

The mythical American male is a loner—a man who can tame the wilderness through his own grit and sweat and determination, a man who doesn't need others to be happy and satisfied. One hundred and sixty years ago, the French sociologist Alexis de Tocqueville toured America and saw that this "individualism," as he called it, could ruin community. In his classic work *Democracy in America,* Tocqueville penned these words about the creeping tentacles of individualism:

Individualism is a calm and considered feeling which disposes each citizen to isolate himself from the mass of his fellows and withdraw into the circle of family and friends; with this little society formed to his taste, he gladly leaves the greater society to look after itself.[2]

And what are the consequences of this isolation and withdrawal?

Each man is forever thrown back on himself alone, and there is danger that he may be shut up in the solitude of his own heart.[3]

Sadly, this is where most men are today—thrown back on themselves and shut up in the solitude of their own hearts. Other than the superficial "hellos" at work and the shallow conversations in the church foyer, many of us are disconnected from this life-giving organism we call "the community of men." We may not realize it, but we're suffering in its absence.

And so are our sons.

Where Boys Become Men

In the Middle Ages, pages and squires became knights because they were part of a masculine community. At an early age, the page left home and entered into a mentoring relationship with an older man, usually a cousin or an uncle. As a squire (ages 14 to 21), the young lad competed in tournaments, perfecting the skills of knighthood. In this environment he was surrounded by men.

Throughout the rest of his life, the community of men admonished, affirmed, and endorsed his masculinity. Life was filled with camaraderie, protection, and high ideals.

Boys become men in the community of men. There is no substitute for this vital component. Dad, if your boy is to become a man, *you must enlist the community.* This is imperative for three reasons.

First, if a father's presence is weighty, the presence of other men is weightier still. It's one thing for my son to sit and listen to his dad talk about manhood; it's another thing entirely for him to hear this same discussion in the presence of a group. A synergism of values, sobriety, and depth takes place when other men are added to the mix.

Sons can sometimes dismiss what they're hearing with the plaintive, "Oh, this is just Dad talking." *But it's not just Dad talking!* The *community* is telling him what is valuable.

Second, enlisting the community of men results in a depth of friendship that the lonely never experience. As meaningful as my relationships have been with Bill Wellons and Bill Parkinson, our ceremonies have taken our friendship to a whole new level. You tend to look at men differently when you know they have a personal stake in the success or failure of your son. I loved these two men dearly before we began our journey; I love them even more today.

And third, the community of men expands a son's spiritual and moral resources. Our sons have begun to relate to the other two fathers in ways we never expected. They seek us out and willingly share their struggles and successes. We ask them how they're doing, and they tell us. Honestly. Openly. Bonded through the mystical power of ceremony, we have become mentors to these young men. The experience has enriched their lives and changed us as well.

If you are serious about moving your son to manhood, begin asking the Lord to lead you to a small community of men. Seek out a group of fathers with sons who will band together with you in the adventure. Form a community. Instill ideals in your boys, create ceremonies, and initiate them into manhood. But do it *together!* Then enjoy the satisfaction of raising a new generation of Modern-Day Knights.

Part V

The Knight and His Legacy

CHAPTER 12

†HE DECREE

We decree that no one shall be knighted
unless he is a knight's son.
—THE CORTES OF CATALONIA (1235)

Jimmy Sorvillo is a member of my church. He recently entered a couple of new stages of life: being a husband and a father. But Jimmy is also something else. He is a success story in manhood.

How did he get that way? I'll let him tell you. Read these words carefully:

> I grew up in a Christian home, where my father played a very
> active role in my life. He worked hard, but never at the
> expense of losing time with me or my family. I feel fortunate
> having listened to the stories of friends and of other men's
> lives. I have been made more aware of what God has truly
> given me. My father has always been there for me.

My grandfather has also been there for me. I remember as
a young boy how my grandfather faithfully came by on Saturday mornings and took my brother and me on outings.

From them, I was taught the meaning of hard work, discipline, absolutes, values, and the true definition of family. In
my dad I have seen modeled the balance between working
hard for a living and still pouring your life into your wife and
children. I have seen a godly man who continues to grow spiritually and takes on leadership positions in the church.

I have also been surrounded by godly men from our
church. These men have not only been examples to me, but
they have also helped me down the road into manhood.
Recently, I married into a family where my wife's father has
been the spiritual leader of his home, too.

God has truly blessed me with a rarity in this day. I am
surrounded by a father, men in the church, and a father-in-law
who have all been godly examples. My story is not one of pain
and sorrow, but one of happiness and thankfulness to our
heavenly Father for what He has given me.

Real manhood in a son never comes by accident. There's an art to it.

As we discovered in Chapter 1, the institution of knighthood arose
in the last half of the Middle Ages. Until the middle of the eleventh
century, the main criterion for admission to the knightly class was
money. According to Frances Gies, "Anyone could belong who could
afford a war-house, armor, equipment, and peasants to work his lands
in his absence."[1] The poor needed not—and did not—apply.

But over time, what was solely a financial barrier also became a
social barrier. After 1050, knighthood was passed *from father to son*,
thereby becoming a privilege determined by heredity. In the thir-

teenth century, legislative bodies throughout Europe began to formalize this practice by restricting knighthood to family birth.

One such declaration was issued by the Cortes (legislature) of Catalonia, the northeast kingdom of Spain. In one sentence, the decree restricted the institution of knighthood. In Latin, the declaration reads: *decrevimus ut nullus nisi filius equitis equestris dignitas habeat.* Translated into English, it means, "We decree that no one shall be knighted unless he is a knight's son."

Did you hear that, Dad? This ancient decree is also a powerful principle of manhood: Only the son of a knight (a real man) can become a knight (a real man).

THE NATURAL PATHWAY

This is the formula missing from so many families today. We expect Modern-Day Knights to somehow emerge from the homes of absent or irresponsible fathers—men whose lives are marked by workaholism, selfishness, and absenteeism. But the Decree says "No." Everyone in medieval society knew that the sons of peasants did not become knights. In modern society, neither do the sons of absent or irresponsible dads.

There are, of course, exceptions to the Decree. Some sons of dysfunctional fathers, by the grace of God, will indeed become godly men. But this alternative path—as I can testify—is strewn with heartache, pain, roadblocks, and work. And for every success story, there are a hundred tragedies.

The Decree highlights the natural pathway—the one Jimmy Sorvillo walked. The chief component in a boy's journey to manhood is Dad: his modeling, his involvement. When a dad exudes these knightly qualities, his son will possess a distinct advantage other sons lack. God, not man, has decreed this (see Deuteronomy 11:18-21).

The Importance of Character

On a snowy day, General Robert E. Lee took his eight-year-old son, Custis, out for a walk. Wearied by the high drifts, Custis began to fall behind his father.

> After a few minutes Lee looked back and found that his boy was behind him, imitating his every move and walking in the tracks the father had made in the snow. "When I saw this," Lee told one of his friends long afterwards, "I said to myself, it behooves me to walk very straight when this fellow is already following in my tracks."[2]

Every dad begins fatherhood with a distinct and awesome advantage: the unstinting admiration of his son. Wise dads, like Lee, recognize their privileged position and build upon it by *modeling* the message they preach to their sons. They know that words are only as strong as the source from which they arise.

Listen to the Decree in a biblical context: "A righteous man who walks in his integrity—how blessed are his sons after him" (Proverbs 20:7).

You might want to pause for a moment and ponder your own life before this revealing passage. Do you want your son to be blessed? This biblical decree says *you* are the key! The sons of a righteous man possess a natural advantage other sons don't.

Unfortunately, many dads waste the "hero" image that was imbued in their sons from birth. Recently, a 20-year-old man at our church shared with me the greatest disappointment of his life. Doug told me what a crushing emotional blow it was to peek into the kitchen late one night and witness his father sneaking long gulps from a bottle of vodka.

Though there had been other disappointments, the sight of his dad staggering through the kitchen sealed in Doug's mind what he had long suspected: His dad was not the man he claimed to be. He was not the knight a son longs to admire. He was a four-letter word every son despises: *fake!* This discovery hurt far more deeply than his father's drunkenness. In that awful moment, the natural leadership of a father with his son was lost.

Listen to Lewis Yablonsky:

> Boys tend to be heavily involved emotionally with their fathers as *role models,* even though they may spend more time with their mothers, sisters and peers. Boys look to their fathers for cues as to how to act out their male roles, and specifically, later on, their roles as fathers [emphasis added].[3]

At this point, let us be as clear and direct as possible: Dad, if you are going to raise a Modern-Day Knight, there is no substitute for your personal character and integrity! By it your son becomes advantaged, empowered, and inspired.

Take a look at this description of a father's knightly character from the pen of a good friend of mine, Lee Burrell:

> Growing up, I remember that my father—a doctor—was there for me. My dad taught me to hunt, to fish, to enjoy the outdoors and sports, to be gentle with people.
>
> I have many rich memories of doing things—fun things, challenging things, quiet things, tedious things—with my dad. But most of all, I remember my dad's life. By it he taught me to appreciate people, to never take them for granted . . . to reach out to those less fortunate than ourselves . . . to refuse bigotry.

He modeled not quitting to me and the value of hard work. He displayed a great deal of patience with me and trust in me. He encouraged me to do my best, while he did the best he could.

So when I reflect upon my childhood and adolescence with my dad, there is much that is pleasant and good that rests there.

Just how important is your integrity? In a comprehensive two-year study of more than 6,000 students, researcher Michael Josephson discovered that 76 percent of high school students and 81 percent of college students listed *parents* as their biggest moral influences.[4] Surprisingly, no one else even came close—not teachers, or coaches, or even peers.

You Are a Role Model

Dad, your son desires more than ideals. He needs more than ceremonies. His heart cries out for a father who *lives* like a knight; a dad who not only knows what he believes, but lives out what he believes.

In 1 Thessalonians 2:10-12, the apostle Paul describes his ministry in Thessalonica: "You are witnesses, and so is God, how devoutly and uprightly and blamelessly we behaved toward you believers; just as you know how we were exhorting and encouraging and imploring each one of you as a father would his own children, so that you would walk in a manner worthy of the God who calls you into His own kingdom and glory."

The Thessalonians were stirred to Christian obedience because Paul exhorted and encouraged and implored them "as a father would his own children." He spoke encouraging words. He raised godly standards. He upheld godly ideals.

But the real strength of Paul's ministry isn't found in verse 11; it's found in verse 10. His words carried weight because *his life* was exemplary. Three adverbs describe the quality of his life. "Devoutly" refers to Paul's *spiritual* life. "Uprightly" refers to *moral* integrity. "Blamelessly" refers to *social* integrity. As he stood before his contemporaries, Paul was much more than a preacher. He was a spiritual Sir Lancelot, wielding the sword of a holy, moral, pure life.

Good fathers exhort and encourage and implore their sons; *great* fathers drive home these messages with their own spiritual, moral, and social integrity. Sons observe Dad in the rough and tumble of life. They watch what *he* watches on television; they observe how *he* treats their mom.

In a thousand different ways, a son absorbs his father's values by witnessing actions, behaviors, and attitudes. The real legacy we leave in our sons' lives is what we have lived out before them. Here, then, is the pressing question for any dad: "Is my lifestyle the stuff of knighthood?"

In the movie *To Kill a Mockingbird,* Gregory Peck plays Atticus Finch, an attorney in a small Southern town. While the story is about race and prejudice, it also conveys a more subtle message: the value of a father's integrity. Throughout the movie, we catch glimpses of Mr. Finch's integrity—but always through the eyes of his children, Jem and Scout.

A black man, Tom Robinson, is wrongly accused of raping a white woman; Atticus defends him at great personal risk. In so doing, he incurs the wrath of the bigoted white community. A white mob descends upon the jail to lynch the defendant; Atticus steps between Tom and the vigilantes, saving Tom's life.

After Tom is convicted of a crime he didn't commit, the courtroom empties and a dejected Atticus walks slowly down the aisle. His daughter, Scout, who has been sitting in the balcony with Tom's friends and family, watches Atticus as he moves toward her. Reverently, the blacks rise to their feet. One of them, the Reverend Sykes, taps Scout on the shoulder and says, "Miss Jean Louise, stand up. Your father's passin'."

Dad, what does your son do when *you* pass by? What does his soul say? Is it inspired and moved by your character? Does he observe truth in your life, in your motives, in your responses? Does his spirit stand up in respect? Does his heart cry out, *I want to be just like my father— the knight?*

Thank God there are exceptions to the Decree. My life is one of them. But exceptions will not heal a land or restore families or redeem a nation. For the Decree proclaims an immovable standard that each generation must never forget: Only the sons of knights become knights!

In the pages of this book, I've endeavored to resurrect the knight: his ideals, his process, his ceremonies, and his community. I've allowed him to speak to a new generation of sons—yours and mine— who also have the potential for virtue and greatness. Now, Dad, it's in your hands. Just remember . . .

The glory of sons is their fathers.

Mason (left), Garrett, and me fishing near Snowmass, Colorado

CHAPTER 13

WHERE THE BOYS ARE

Nothing so encourages a man like results.

—ANONYMOUS

I t was 1989 when my friends Bill Wellons, Bill Parkinson, and I first committed ourselves to raise our sons together. Honestly, we weren't even sure what we were committing *to*. We just knew we needed each other's help and encouragement as young, inexperienced dads.

At the time, our seven sons spanned preschool through college. Our oldest—Bill Parkinson, Jr.—was 19. Our youngest—my son, Mason—was 3.

The big, hairy question before us was this: How does a dad mold a boy into a man—a real man, one he and God can be proud of?

It was clear that our boys needed something more than we'd been giving them. We sensed it revolved around a better-defined direction, a vision for their lives that we were unsure of ourselves.

Since life was speeding up, not slowing down, we knew we needed answers right away. So together we set out to find them.

That was 18 years ago. Our sons are no longer tearing up the house, shooting baskets in the driveway, or playing Nintendo with friends in the living room while cheese dip flies everywhere. We're no longer driving to every little town in Arkansas to watch them play football, basketball, baseball, and soccer.

They're gone, all of them—gone into life, careers, marriages, and having kids of their own.

When Focus on the Family called about updating this book, the folks there asked, "Where are the boys now?" The question was a good one. After all, when *Raising a Modern-Day Knight* was first published in 1997, we were still constructing and polishing our "boys-to-men" model. Good things were happening, but the final results weren't in.

The bottom line of life isn't just faith; it's the results of faith. Years ago I was captured by a line from singer/songwriter Paul Simon: "Faith is an island in the setting sun, but proof, proof is the bottom line for everyone." I couldn't agree more. As my mom used to say, "The proof is in the pudding."

The original version of *Raising a Modern-Day Knight* is about three dads seeking to guide their seven sons to authentic manhood. The version you hold includes results. In Paul Harvey's words, it's "the rest of the story."

As I write this, our boys are men between the ages of 21 and 37. What's happened to them? What kind of impact did our efforts make?

In the short letter of 3 John, the apostle makes a striking statement:

> For I was very glad when brethren came and testified to your truth, that is, how you are walking in truth. I have no greater

joy than this, to hear of my children walking in the truth. (3 John 3-4)

I had a moment of joy like that recently. It was at Ben Wellons' manhood ceremony. My only regret is that I have only one picture—a posed one—which includes only some of us from that special gathering.

It was on this occasion that we inducted Ben into our community of men. Five sons and two sons-in-law had preceded him. Tonight, Ben was to be given his manhood ring. But first each man had an opportunity to speak manhood truth into Ben's life.

As I watched dads and sons speak from their hearts to Ben, I couldn't help but recall the apostle John's words. Our sons were all walking in truth.

Front row (left to right): Brent James (my son-in-law); Bill Parkinson; Garrett Lewis; Bill Parkinson, Jr. Back Row (left to right): Fred Wood (Bill Wellons' son-in-law); Bill Wellons, Jr.; Ben Wellons; Bill Wellons; me

What joy could top this for a dad? Good grades? A state championship? A college scholarship? A good job? None could come even close.

Our sons and sons-in-law were all expressing their manhood in Jesus Christ. It wasn't forced or coerced; it was sincere and passionate. For a dad, it was the deepest kind of joy.

I wasn't just glorying in our sons. I was glorying in a loving God and the gracious help He'd given us dads in raising our boys. It had been a long and sometimes bumpy road. But here, tonight, the proof was surely in the pudding. Glory to God!

BILL PARKINSON'S SONS

So, where are our sons now? Let me start with Bill Parkinson's three sons—Bill, Jr., Ben, and Daniel.

Bill, Jr. was 19 when we three dads began to get our act together. Part of our wake-up call came when Bill, Jr. lost a good bit of his faith—and his way—during college.

Daniel, Ben, and Bill Parkinson, Jr.

Shortly after he graduated from college, we three dads invited Bill, Jr. to dinner. He was working as a waiter in Little Rock, struggling with feelings of failure. He had no idea we were going to call him to manhood that night and honor him with our first manhood ring.

To this day, he says that evening was a turning point for him. He found there were men who still believed in him—not just his dad, but others, too. Instead of giving up on him, we stood with him. That night he heard for the first time a vision for how to turn his life around.

So powerful was this evening that a short time later he asked his dad to write down all we'd said to him. He didn't want to forget any of it.

Bill, Jr. later joined a small group of men under a wise mentor, Jim Strawn, to explore more fully what biblical manhood is all about. Significant, positive changes followed. Today, at 37, Bill, Jr. is president of Parkinson Building Group, a residential construction company. He and his wife, Jessica, have three children—Witt, Caroline, and Thomas.

Then there was Bill's younger brother Ben. He'd received much more manhood input from us while going through high school. As a student at Baylor, Ben became very involved in campus ministry; it became clear that he has strong spiritual leadership gifts.

At his wedding rehearsal dinner, we three dads challenged Ben to use his early twenties to explore spiritual opportunities—and he did. Fresh out of college, he took a year of intensive discipleship training and later attended Dallas Seminary. Today he serves as a teaching pastor at Fellowship Bible Church in Memphis, Tennessee. He and his wife, Aimee, have three children—Abigail, Anna, and Allie.

Daniel, like Ben, had significant exposure to our manhood instruction and ceremonies as he grew up. He was very open about the impact it made in his life. After he and his dad attended a manhood seminar I did for the men of our church, he asked a question I'll never forget: "How would a young man ever figure this out on his own?"

What a great question! The answer, of course, is that a young man can't. Alone, he'll flounder and fail. Thankfully, Daniel learned that early.

Daniel is 30 at this writing. He lives in Houston, Texas, where he works as an account manager for Carlton-Bates, a distributor of electrical and electronic components.

BILL WELLONS' SONS

Bill Wellons would say he's seen his sons benefit equally from our commitment as dads to raise our boys together. In Bill's words, "It has called us all, fathers and sons, to a higher manhood."

Bill's eldest son, Bill, Jr., was always known as a "make it happen" young man. He did that when he helped start a Christian fraternity at Texas Christian University; he did it in a highly entrepreneurial business career. But what he learned about authentic manhood most shaped *how* those things happened. Our manhood instruction led him to several "defining moments" clarifying how to live his life, what to live for, and how to lead his family.

Today Bill, Jr., 32, is a pastor at Fellowship Bible Church in Nashville, Tennessee. He also directs the men's ministry there. He and his wife, Hillary, have three children—Lily, Emma, and Witt.

Ben Wellons, like his brother, feels blessed by our investment in his life. After his manhood ceremony, he said, "This is the most awesome experience I've ever had. Having the men I respect most speaking into my life is incredible." Ben has allowed other men to challenge him spiritually, too. One in particular, Wes Hall, stirred in Ben an evangelistic gift, which the latter now uses to connect other young men to Christ.

At 25, Ben is president of E-Med America, a web-based medical company in Little Rock.

MY SONS

I've had wonderful times with my older son, Garrett, during this Modern-Day Knight process. The ceremonies in particular have been great memory makers.

In Chapter 8 I described the first ceremony I did with Garrett when he was 13. Here's what he most remembers about this event: "My dad spoke to me for the first time like a man instead of a boy. And it felt good."

For me, the ceremony I did with Garrett when he turned 16 was most memorable. He was struggling with life as a high school sophomore, obviously needing an infusion of encouragement and vision. Athletically, he seemed stuck on the bench; school was "boring"; some of his friends were dumping him. Being a preacher's kid didn't help, either.

So I created an "Affirmation Ceremony" designed to remind him of his best qualities and to encourage him to keep pursuing manhood.

To this ceremony I invited three of his closest friends and Mark DeYmaz, his youth pastor. We met at a favorite restaurant under the pretense of celebrating Garrett's sixteenth birthday; after a lively meal, each of his friends spoke a special word to him. I'd asked each to write a page about what he admired most in Garrett.

I will never forget that night.

As comments were read, it became clear that each person had taken this assignment very seriously. The words fed my son's parched soul. Tears filled all our eyes; when my turn came, I had trouble speaking. This is what I said:

To Robert Garrett Lewis on His Sixteenth Birthday

Garrett, I have picked this site to celebrate your sixteenth birthday because it holds such a special memory for you and me.

It was here that we began your journey into manhood. It was here I shared with you the definition of what it means to be a man and asked you to join me in that pursuit of rejecting passivity, accepting responsibility, leading courageously, and expecting God's greater reward. It was here we stuffed ourselves silly and laughed all the way home with our belts unbuckled for breathing room. It was, and will forever be, a special night.

Garrett, I love you. I am proud to call you my son. God has blessed you with many admirable qualities that I want you to know are gifts from God.

You have an excellent mind—the best in the family. It can remember and recall vast amounts of information, as anyone in the Lewis family will attest.

You have a sensitive spirit. You feel for people and can easily enter their successes or pain without regard to yourself. That's a rare quality. Few know, as I know, what a loyal friend you are and will be to those around you.

You have a heart for God. You want to please Him. Nevertheless, carving out your own faith when your dad is a pastor is not easy because you need your own identity. But I have noticed in a number of ways you managing this extra-difficult pursuit. God, I have no doubt, is proud of how well you have done. It is Him, not me, you want to please with your life.

Finally, Garrett, you have a love for sports. In this, you and I have shared many, many special moments. None, however, approach our connection with Larry Bird. Perhaps it is because we love his overachieving spirit, his work ethic, his making the most of what he had, or just the fact that he brought together a father and son around hours of pure fun. Whatever, tonight . . . on your sixteenth birthday, I thought this gift would be a fitting symbol for my challenge to you.

[I then presented Garrett with an autographed picture of Larry Bird.]

Larry Bird represents a commitment to excellence. His life of achievement challenges you and me in the best use of what God has given us, no matter how big or little that is. So, in that light, I want to issue you three challenges:

Because God has made you smart . . . develop your mind to the fullest. Let it open up to you worlds that many people will never know about. Pursue the best with your mind and it and God will reward you.

Because God has made you loyal and sensitive . . . make it your goal to know God personally. The more you know God, the more you understand the ways of God . . . the more you, Garrett, will be able to make the most of your gifts of loyalty and sensitivity. You will learn how to be loyal to the right things and make the wisest use of your sensitive heart. Everyone around you will be blessed by you if you do.

Finally, because God has given you a love of sports . . . make the most of these next few years. Push yourself. Set goals. Work to be the best. Don't let any obstacle—fear, lack of apparent progress, the "lure" of lesser things—keep you from being the best you can be. That's all you can ask of yourself, Garrett. But, Garrett, ask nothing less. This is what sports best teaches. So go for it, in Larry Bird style.

I love you, son. Regardless of what life holds, I will never, ever stop loving you.

You are my son in whom I am well pleased.—Dad

I really believe this affirmation steadied my son's life when he needed it most. Things didn't get easier right away; they actually got harder. But Garrett took my three challenges and pressed forward. His senior year he was a captain of his football team. He later won a full academic scholarship to college, where he played for the Arkansas Razorbacks.

Today Garrett, 25, lives in Little Rock. He's studying to be a doctor.

My younger son, Mason, has also connected over the years to the manhood vision this book has presented. As with Garrett, Mason and I have used this process to relate more deeply as father and son.

Probably the most powerful manhood moment for Mason and me came as he was completing high school. I invited four of his friends and their dads to be part of his "Squire Stage Ceremony."

For six weeks before the ceremony, participants met at my home every Monday morning at 6:30 to discuss how to be successful at college. As we looked to God's Word for help, every son was challenged to set two goals for his college years in these areas: academic life, spiritual life, friends, girls, and great experiences to be had. It was one of the best, most productive times I've ever had with Mason.

The ceremony itself was a celebration dinner at the Capitol Hotel. Everyone came in coat and tie. After dinner, each son stood and shared his college goals. Then we dads blessed our sons, prayed over

The Squire Stage manhood ceremony for Mason and his friends. From left: Jim Greenwald, Drew Johnson, Frank Ramey, Walker Bowden, me, Mason, Taylor Ramey, Dale Johnson, Peyton Greenwald.

them, and presented them with black "reminder bands" which read, "Without a vision, a man will get out of control. Proverbs 29:18."

We had fun, too. After the ceremony we all went to a bowling alley, still dressed in suit and tie, to participate in what we called "The World Championship Suit Bowling Games." We looked ridiculous, but what a great time!

As I write this, Mason is a 21-year-old sophomore at the University of Arkansas. A strong leader who loves people, he's meeting his goals and loving college life. Recently he organized a group of students to help with disaster relief in New Orleans after Hurricane Katrina. He also has a big heart for sharing Christ with his peers.

So this is where our boys are now. They're all very different, but linked by a common vision—a vision of manhood centered in Jesus Christ.

God has taken all three of us dads far beyond our wildest dreams. He's taken our shaky commitment to be better fathers, and our groping in the dark for direction, and turned it into a powerful vision for our sons. Our boys' faith is now their own. I can only express my feelings by using the words of Paul in Ephesians 3:20-21 (NIV):

> Now to him who is able to do immeasurably more than all we
> ask or imagine, according to his power that is at work within
> us, to him be glory in the church and in Christ Jesus through-
> out all generations, for ever and ever! Amen.

AND THE LEGACY GOES ON

Recently Bill, Bill, and I were privileged to participate in a next-generation Modern-Day Knight event. Fred Wood (Bill Wellons' son-in-law), Bill Parkinson, Jr., and other dads had joined to take their preteen sons through the six-part *Raising a Modern-Day Knight Video Adventure Series*, which I did with Dennis Rainey. (For more information on this video curriculum, go to www.RMDK.com.)

This program includes a "Dads' Commitment Ceremony" with swords, candles, and pageantry. Sons are invited to watch their dads commit to one another and to God to be the kind of fathers their sons need to grow up strong, healthy, and filled with manhood vision. You simply had to be there to feel the power of this event. Clearly the sons were in awe as they watched their dads make the following pledge:

> I, [dad], before God, commit myself to raise you, [son], to be a
> Modern-Day Knight. I promise to love you, impart God's wis-
> dom to you, spend time with you, have fun with you, and be
> the strategic dad you need me to be. I promise to lead you into
> the masculinity of the Second Adam, Jesus Christ. So help me
> God. Amen.

Bill, Bill, and me celebrating fatherhood with dads Bruce Henry (left), Bill Wellons' son-in-law Fred Wood (middle), Bill Parkinson, Jr. (right) and their sons

As I stood with Bill and Bill, watching "our men" begin the process of launching authentic manhood into a third generation, I couldn't help but utter these words: "Lord Jesus, thank You for letting me see this day."

CHAPTER 14

A Word to Dads Who Think They Blew It

He will restore the hearts of the fathers to their
children and the hearts of the children to their fathers. . . .
—MALACHI 4:6

There are few things as bitter as regret. It shadows life with a persistent, painful message of "what could have been." I've seen the dark eyes of regret in hundreds of dads over the years in the Men's Fraternity meetings I've had the privilege of leading.

Men's Fraternity, a program I started in 1990, helps men discover and establish a more confident, competent, and God-honoring lifestyle. (You can learn more about it at www.mensfraternity.com.) It explores and dissects many subjects, including a man's work, his relationship with a woman, his unique design, developing a satisfying life focus, sex, money, marriage—and parenting.

It's when I talk about that last topic, especially about the father-son relationship, that regret often raises its head. After I describe what a son needs from his dad, a number of men will step forward, surround me, and one by one make a common confession I could summarize with three statements:

"I missed it with my boy."

"I wish I had heard this ____ years ago."

"Is there anything I can do now?"

Maybe you're a dad like that. You've read this book, only to be filled with remorse by nagging reflections of what might have been. Or maybe someone gave you the book—and as you surveyed the table of contents, this last chapter caught your eye. Regret led you to start reading here, and to ask, "Is there any hope for me with my son? Is there anything I can do to recover lost ground?"

The answer, I'm happy to say, is "Yes." It may require some hard humility on your part, but I can declare with certainty that as long as you're both alive, it's never too late to close the gap with your son. *Never.*

No matter what the distance or damage, sons have a remarkable readiness to reconnect with their fathers *if approached rightly.* Author Lance Morrow put it this way: "The longing of sons for their fathers is something passionate and profound. It is almost physical."[1]

BUDDY'S STORY

Buddy Griffin is one example. I met him at a Men's Fraternity workshop in Houston.

Buddy was 64. You wouldn't think of him as a son needing his father, but the truth is that Buddy's whole life had been affected by the loss he felt over never having connected with his dad.

"My father never told me he loved me," Buddy said to me. "I

could never please him or measure up to his expectation." Where love should have been, there was only deep anger and resentment. You could hear it in Buddy's voice.

Yet Buddy was talking to me about this bitterness because he still needed and wanted a relationship with his dad. In spite of his father's shortcomings, Buddy still longed for his dad's love and approval. For a son, this primal desire *never* goes away.

I challenged Buddy to take a courageous step—to go to his dad and ask for his love and a hug. At first Buddy resisted. "I can't do that. Besides, my dad is 94 years old and in a nursing home. Nothing is going to change now."

Despite Buddy's protests, I persisted in my request. I'll let him tell you what happened next.

Exactly a week later, I asked Jim Laucher, a dear friend of mine, to go visit my dad with me so he could pray for me and provide moral support. As I entered my dad's apartment, I felt like a five year old. After a brief "How are you?" visit, I said to him, "Dad, I need to tell you something you might not understand. I really need you to tell me you love me."

He responded, "I love everybody."

I said, "Dad, no . . . I want you to tell me!"

He hesitated and finally said in a low tone, "I love you."

I quickly responded, "Dad, I want you to say it in a loud voice so I can hear it really good." I could tell this was difficult for him but he finally did.

Then I said, "Dad, I need for you to hug me!" I made him stand up and he gave me a brief, sideways hug with one arm.

I responded, "Dad, I need a real hug. Put your arms around me and hug me."

He did and immediately said, "I have to go."

Before he turned to leave, though, I told him that every time I came to see him in the future I wanted us to do the same thing. He walked out of the room.

As Jim and I left, he was praising our Lord and slapping me on the back with "Way to go's."

I felt such relief!

I have gone to see my dad many times since then. Each time gets better and better. Now when I walk into his apartment, he expects the hugs and words of love and actually enjoys it! So do I! Finally, after all these years, my 94-year-old dad and I, his 64-year-old son, have a neat father-son relationship . . . just like it should be!

When I bury my father, I can now stand there with no regrets. Praise God!

Why is this story so important to you as a dad?

Because you can be assured that whatever has happened (or not happened) between you and your son, under all those layers of hurt and distance he longs to be reconnected to you. To forgive you. To be right with you. To start over.

Let me say it again: It is never too late to build a right relationship with your son. You can't go back, but you can go forward. And sons desperately want to go forward.

The Prodigal Dad

The story Jesus told of the prodigal son in Luke 15 shows how powerful the father-son relationship is—and how forgiving it can be when things are done right.

The story begins with the son doing everything wrong. He's selfish, ungrateful, greedy, and demanding. Completely self-absorbed and rebellious, he takes his share of his father's estate and squanders it on decadent pleasure and everything alien to his father's values.

Yet, when he comes to his senses (verse 17), repents, and returns humble and contrite to his father's house, an amazing thing happens.

His father lets the past go.

There are no "I told you so's" or "You owe me's" or "Let me tell you how you've hurt me's." The joy of renewing the father-son relationship trumps all that.

Nowhere in the story is that seen more powerfully than as the father waits on the doorstep for his wayward son to appear. At the first glimpse of his return, Jesus said, the father "ran and embraced him and kissed him" (verse 20).

I believe the father-son bond is so compelling that what works for prodigal sons also works for prodigal fathers. Sons yearn to run to their wayward dads. They wait for their dads to "come home" and set things right—whether the issue is neglect, absenteeism, verbal or physical abuse, lack of approval, a critical spirit, divorce, anger, hypocrisy, emotional abandonment, or plain old incompetence.

I believe *your* son is waiting.

RIGHT MOVES

Regardless of where you and your son are, there are three moves you can make with God's help (never forget to pray and ask for His help). Some of this will be scary and require courage on your part. But don't let fear hold you back. Keep your eye on the prize—an open, loving relationship with your son.

Here are the three practical steps you can take. I've seen them work.

Step 1: Interview Him

You can restart your relationship with your son by going to him with a fresh commitment to a new beginning. Pulling this off will require two important ingredients from you: real humility and a deep desire for understanding.

When meeting with your son, share your heart—including your love and whatever regret you have over not being the kind of dad you know you should have been. Tell your son how you've come to this insight (books, small group studies, seminars, etc.) and how it's affected you. Open your heart wide to him. Tell him you want to be a good dad for him from this point on, but that you'll need his help in knowing how.

Then *interview* your son.

Without defensive comebacks, excuses, or justifications, ask him how you can be a better dad. Then *listen*. It might help to have a pen and paper to record some of his comments.

To stimulate your son's thinking, you might ask questions like these:

"What are the one or two things you need most from me as a dad?"

"What would be the most encouraging thing I could do for you right now?"

"What do I need to stop doing?"

"If you could change one thing about me as a dad, what would it be?"

"What's one thing I need to make up to you in our relationship?"

As your son responds to these questions, you might have to encourage him to elaborate so that you fully understand. But don't leave until you "get it"—all of it.

After asking these questions and listening (not reacting) to your son's answers, thank him for his time and honesty. Tell him you'll think deeply about the responses he gave you. Let him know that from this point on, you'll do everything you can to be the dad he needs.

I've seen this interview process work many times in restarting a relationship between father and son. Most often, a son is stunned that his father would take such a step. Dad's humility is the great door opener.

I remember one dad who took me up on this. A hardworking businessman, he'd come to regret the long hours he spent at the office, away from his family. "I missed so much," he said tearfully. "Ball games, campouts, everything. I was completely absent."

His son, now 32, was about to complete his residency in internal medicine. "It's time for a restart!" I said.

After further discussion, my friend bought a plane ticket and flew to see his son. The two of them had lunch and spent a long afternoon together. Through it all, the dad kept expressing his desire to be a better father and asking his son how.

When that dad got back home, his wife told him she'd just talked to their son on the phone.

"What did he say?" the father asked anxiously.

His wife replied, "Our son said he finally had his dad's attention, and it was the best day of his life!"

STEP 2: CONFESS TO HIM

You can restore your relationship with your son by confessing your sin against him and seeking his forgiveness.

Sin is an awful wedge. It can keep a dad and son apart for a lifetime. One ugly word or act that you as a dad refuse to own up to can keep your son away even as he longs to be with you.

Is that you? If you're at odds with your son, what stands between you? Could you name it? Do you own it? Part of it?

James says directly, "Therefore, confess your sins to one another, and pray for one another so that you may be healed" (James 5:16). He doesn't say, "Wait for the other guy to confess his sin before you confess yours."

James is asking you and me to account for our words and deeds—in this case, the ones that have hurt our sons. If we've hurt or offended our sons directly or indirectly, it would be courageous to own up to it, call it what it is—a sin, and seek forgiveness.

This is, of course, a good lifetime practice for all dads. Certainly asking forgiveness is a "best practice" of all the great dads I know. But for dads who've blown it with their sons, and in their sin have inflicted significant relational damage, seeking forgiveness is a must. Otherwise your unconfessed sin will poison your relationship with your son and prevent it from ever having the spirited connection God meant fathers and sons to have.

For over 15 years I watched one dad try in vain to convince his sons that divorcing their mom had been justifiable. It wasn't that he openly slandered his ex-wife; it's just that when the boys would bring up the divorce, he would say to them things like, "We just weren't made for one another"; "We were better off going our separate ways"; "I just wasn't the right person for your mother." Then he would try to win the boys over with fun times together. But as he confessed to me later, "The boys and I never bonded. There was always a distant coolness between us, which at times turned to anger."

I suggested he address the issue head-on. I asked, "As a Christian, do you think it was right for you to divorce your wife?"

After a long pause, he said, "No."

I asked, "Why don't you tell that to your boys *and* to your ex-wife and ask their forgiveness?"

He told me he wasn't sure he could do that. But several months later he did. He poured out his heart to his sons and admitted his wrong, just as James instructed. Then he humbly asked their forgiveness. Almost instantly he felt from his sons a warmth and closeness no amount of money or excuses could buy.

I'm reminded of what God said through the prophet Joel: "Return to Me with all your heart. . . . Then I will make up to you for the years that the swarming locust has eaten" (Joel 2:12, 25). In his brokenness, that dad learned firsthand that God still delivers on that promise.

STEP 3: BLESS HIM

You can re-energize your relationship with your son by blessing him.

Every son needs his father's blessing. Sons who don't get that blessing will always feel a sense of incompleteness. If you're a dad who has regrets, this may be the single most important thing you can do for your son after years of conflict or neglect. He needs you to bless him!

Scripture reminds us, "Death and life are in the power of the tongue" (Proverbs 18:21). Blessing your son has a special, life-giving power all its own. God's first words to His children, Adam and Eve, were in the form of a blessing (Genesis 1:28). All through the Bible we see dads blessing their sons (see Genesis 49:28, for example).

Interestingly, the only recorded, spoken words of God to His Son, Jesus, while the latter was on earth were words of blessing: "This is My beloved Son, in whom I am well-pleased" (Matthew 3:17). If Jesus as a son needed to be blessed, then it's no stretch to say all sons need a blessing.

Bill Glass was one of the most outstanding football players in the NFL during the 1960s, playing for the Cleveland Browns. In 1969 he began a prison ministry called Champions for Life. After 36 years in that ministry, he was asked by *Christianity Today*, "What is our country's biggest problem?"

Glass's answer was to the point: "A lack of the father's blessing."

Glass went on to say, "I've got two boys, 280 and 290 pounds. One played pro ball and both played college ball and are bigger than I am, but I grabbed that eldest son of mine recently and said, 'I love you, I bless you, I think you're terrific, and I'm so glad you're mine!' His shoulders began to shake and his eyes filled with tears and he said, 'Dad, I really needed that!'"[2]

Yes, Dad, your blessing is that important and powerful! Your son needs to be blessed by you. Has he? Have you passionately spoken into his life, eyeball to eyeball, words of blessing to him—how much he means to you, how special he is to you, how much you love him, and how unique and treasured his attributes are?

Regardless of what has happened or not happened between you and your son, giving your son your blessing will energize his life. It may also reenergize your relationship and pave the way for better days with him. Bless your son, Dad. And keep blessing him throughout your life.

PRESS ON

You may have blown it with your son in the past. But as long as the two of you are breathing, you have a second chance. Your story as a dad *is not finished.* Believe that.

Your son is waiting for you—waiting to forgive you, to get right with you, to be reconnected at a heart level to you.

God is also waiting—with the power to turn your regret into joy.

Everyone is waiting.

It's your move, Dad.

Notes

CHAPTER 1

1. Robert A. Caro, *The Years of Lyndon Johnson: The Path to Power* (New York: Vintage, 1983), 309.
2. Robert Bly, from the video *A Gathering of Men*, with Bill Moyers, which aired on PBS. The video is available from Mystic Fire Video, P.O. Box 1092, Cooper Station, New York, NY 10276.
3. Frances Gies, *The Knight in History* (New York: Harper & Row, 1984), 206.
4. Richard Barber, *The Knight and Chivalry* (Totowa, N.J.: Rowman and Littlefield, 1975), 44.
5. Julek Heller and Dierdre Headon, *Knights* (New York: Shocken, 1982), 38.
6. Matthew Bennett, "The Knight Unmasked," *The Quarterly Journal of Military History*, vol. 7, no. 4 (Summer 1995): 10.
7. Will and Ariel Durant, *The Story of Civilization—The Age of Faith* 4 (New York: Simon & Schuster, 1950), 578.

CHAPTER 3

1. Lionel Dahmer, *A Father's Story* (New York: William Morrow, 1994), 60.
2. Bronislaw Malinowski, "All in the Family," *National Review* (March 6, 1995): 37.
3. David Blankenhorn, *Fatherless America* (New York: Basic, 1995), 49.
4. Victor Hugo, from *Harper's Book of Quotations*, Robert I. Fitzhenry, ed. (New York: Harper & Row, 1983), 99.

5. Francis Brown, *The New Hebrew and English Lexicon* (Peabody, MA.: Hendrickson, 1979), 802.

6. Richard Hoffer, "What Bo Knows Now," *Sports Illustrated* (October 5, 1995): 56.

7. Gary Graff, "New Wife, Child Give Rocker Bob Seger's Life Focus," *Arkansas Democrat* (October 27, 1994), Section E, 8.

8. Lewis Yablonsky, *Fathers and Sons* (New York: Simon & Schuster, 1982), 27.

9. Allan Bloom, *The Closing of the American Mind* (New York: Simon & Schuster, 1987), 58.

CHAPTER 4

1. Georges Duby, *William Marshall: The Flower of Chivalry* (New York: Pantheon, 1985), 25-26.

2. Sidney Painter, *William Marshall: Knight-Errant, Baron, and Regent of England* (Toronto: University of Toronto Press, 1982), 110-111.

3. Duby, *William Marshall*, 128.

4. Ibid., 75.

5. Found at the Web site of the Bureau of Justice Statistics, U.S. Department of Justice, Office of Justice Programs (http://www.ojp.usdoj.gov/bjs/crimoff.htm).

6. Margaret Mead, *Male and Female: A Study of the Sexes in a Changing World* (New York: Morrow, 1949), quoted from the paperback (New York: Dell, 1968), 168.

7. George Gilder, *Men and Marriage* (Gretna, LA.: Pelican, 1992), 34.

8. David Blankenhorn, *Fatherless America* (New York: Basic, 1995), 17.

9. Gordon Dalbey, *Father and Son* (Nashville: Thomas Nelson, 1992), 4-5.

10. Walter W. Benjamin, "Fatherless Heaven, Fatherless Children," *The Wall Street Journal* (August 16, 1995): 3.

11. Herman Ridderbos, *Paul: An Outline of His Theology* (Grand Rapids, MI: Wm. B. Eerdmans, 1975), 60-61.

12. Stephen B. Clark, *Man and Woman in Christ*, 639.

13. Ibid.

14. Tom Minnery, "A Letter to Dad," *Focus on the Family Citizen*, vol. 9, no. 6 (June 19, 1995): 6.

CHAPTER 5

1. James P. Lenfestey, "Catch of a Lifetime," *Reader's Digest* (February 1989): 111-112.

2. William Kilpatrick, *Why Johnny Can't Tell Right from Wrong* (New York: Simon & Schuster, 1992), 252.

3. Barbara W. Tuchman, *A Distant Mirror* (New York: Ballantine, 1978), 64.

4. Georges Duby, *William Marshall: The Flower of Chivalry* (New York: Pantheon, 1985), 87.

5. Frances Gies, *The Knight in History* (New York: Harper & Row, 1984), 207.

6. Richard Halverson, "A Day at a Time."

7. Gies, *The Knight in History*, 77.

8. Charles F. Boyd, *Different Children, Different Needs* (Sisters, OR.: Multnomah, 1994), 19. Boyd's book is an indispensable tool for identifying your child's strengths and abilities.

9. Gies, *The Knight in History*, 78.

CHAPTER 6

1. Mike Boettcher, "Hell in the Pacific," *Dateline*, NBC News, August 4, 1995.
2. Will Durant, *The Story of Civilization—Caesar and Christ* 3 (New York: Simon & Schuster, 1944), 622.
3. Will and Ariel Durant, *The Story of Civilization—The Age of Napoleon* 11 (New York: Simon & Schuster, 1975), 111.
4. Will and Ariel Durant, *The Story of Civilization—The Age of Faith* 4 (New York: Simon & Schuster, 1950), 293.
5. Gail Sheehy, *Pathfinders* (New York: William Morrow, 1981), 12.
6. Ernest Becker, *The Denial of Death* (New York: Free Press, 1973), 6.
7. William Damon, *Greater Expectations* (New York: Free Press, 1995), 81.

CHAPTER 7

1. Will and Ariel Durant, *The Story of Civilization—The Age of Faith* 4 (New York: Simon & Schuster, 1950), 572-573.
2. Richard Barber, *The Knight and Chivalry* (Totowa, N.J.: Rowman and Littlefield, 1975), 38.
3. Fyodor Dostoevsky, *The Brothers Karamazov*, Andrew R. MacAndrew, trans. (New York: Bantam, 1970), 934.

CHAPTER 8

1. Garry Wills, *Lincoln at Gettysburg: The Words That Remade America* (New York: Simon & Schuster, 1992), 21.
2. Ibid., 34.
3. A book that helped us in creating our crest is *The Oxford Guide to Heraldry*, by Thomas Woodcock and John Martin Robinson (New York: Oxford, 1988). It is available in most

public libraries. *A Complete Guide to Heraldry* by Arthur Charles Fox-Davies (New York: Gramercy, 1978) is also useful. Both books detail hundreds of examples of ancient crests, explaining symbolism and history.

4. James C. Dobson, *Parenting Isn't for Cowards* (Dallas: Word, 1987), 143.

5. Jay Parini, *John Steinbeck: A Biography* (New York: Henry Holt, 1995), 25.

6. William S. McFeely, *Grant: A Biography* (New York: W. W. Norton, 1982), xii.

CHAPTER 10

1. C. Samuel Storms, *Reaching God's Ear* (Wheaton, IL.: Tyndale, 1988), 151.

2. Alfred Edersheim, *The Life and Times of Jesus the Messiah* (McLean, VA.: MacDonald, 1971), 281.

CHAPTER 11

1. Peter Laslett, "The World We Have Lost," *Man Alone: Alienation in Modern Society,* eds. Eric and Mary Josephson (New York: Dell, 1970), 93.

2. Cited in *Habits of the Heart,* ed. Robert N. Bellah (New York: Harper & Row, 1985), 37.

3. Ibid.

CHAPTER 12

1. Frances Gies, *The Knight in History* (New York: Harper & Row, 1984), 25.

2. Douglas Southall Freeman, *R. E. Lee* vol. I (New York: Macmillan, 1934), 178.

3. Lewis Yablonsky, *Fathers and Sons*, 13.

4. Garry Abrams, "Study Finds Young Generation of Americans Light on Morals," *The Arkansas Democrat* (November 13, 1992): section IA.

CHAPTER 14

1. Lance Morrow, as quoted in Allan C. Carlson's article, "What's Wrong with Hillary Clinton's 'It Takes a Village'," *Civilization* (January-February 1996), 30.

2. Nancy Madsen, "The Power of a Father's Blessing," *Christianity Today*, vol. 50, no. 1 (January 2006), 48.

FOCUS ON THE FAMILY®

Welcome to the Family

Whether you purchased this book, borrowed it, or received it as a gift, thanks for reading it! This is just one of many insightful, biblically based resources that Focus on the Family produces for people in all stages of life.

Focus is a global Christian ministry dedicated to helping families thrive as they celebrate and cultivate God's design for marriage and experience the adventure of parenthood. Our outreach exists to support individuals and families in the joys and challenges they face, and to equip and empower them to be the best they can be.

Through our many media outlets, we offer help and hope, promote moral values and share the life-changing message of Jesus Christ with people around the world.

Focus on the Family
MAGAZINES

These faith-building, character-developing publications address the interests, issues, concerns, and challenges faced by every member of your family from preschool through the senior years.

For More
INFORMATION

ONLINE:
Log on to
FocusOnTheFamily.com
In Canada, log on to
FocusOnTheFamily.ca

PHONE:
Call toll-free:
**800-A-FAMILY
(232-6459)**
In Canada, call toll-free:
800-661-9800

THRIVING FAMILY®	**FOCUS ON**	**FOCUS ON**	**FOCUS ON**
Marriage & Parenting	**THE FAMILY**	**THE FAMILY**	**THE FAMILY**
	CLUBHOUSE JR.®	**CLUBHOUSE®**	**CITIZEN®**
	Ages 4 to 8	Ages 8 to 12	U.S. news issues

Rev. 3/11

More expert resources
for marriage and parenting . . .

Do you want to be a better parent? Enjoy a stronger marriage? Focus on the Family's collection of inspiring, practical, resources can help your family grow closer and stronger than ever before. Whichever format you might need—video, audio, book or e-book, we have something for you. Visit our online Family Store and discover how we can help your family thrive at **FocusOnTheFamily.com/resources**.